13 Most Haunted

CEMETERIES IN MASSACHUSETTS

Sam Baltrusis

978-1725905825
13 Most Haunted Cemeteries in Massachusetts
Sam Baltrusis

13 Most Haunted
CEMETERIES IN MASSACHUSETTS

Sam Baltrusis

Cover photo by Frank C. Grace, Trig Photography
First published 2018

Manufactured in the United States

ISBN 978-1725905825

Library of Congress CIP data applied for.

CONTENTS

ACKNOWLEDGEMENTS

When I wrote my first book, *Ghosts of Boston*, I lived in a haunted Victorian triple-decker with a ghost that I quickly learned was a seamstress. She had an affinity for scissors and my roommate and I would find them moved all over the house. I jokingly called her "scissor sister" after one night a pair mysteriously started to spin on the table. Oddly, I was close to her. Yes, I know that's weird. I ended up leaving that haunted house in Somerville but I considered her my ghostly muse.

Nine books and six years later I stepped out for a coffee after putting the finishing touches on *13 Most Haunted Cemeteries in Massachusetts* in my non-haunted apartment in Somerville's Assembly Row. I came back and noticed two pairs of scissors on my table which I didn't remember taking out of the drawer. I didn't think anything of it until one pair mysteriously made a noise and then fell to the ground while I was writing late at night.

Is she back? Hopefully, the seamstress was just checking in and not planning to set up shop in my one-bedroom apartment. Sorry scissor sister. But there's not enough room for the both of us.

Similar to my experience in 2012 with the seamstress, I became close with one of the spirits featured in *13 Most Haunted Cemeteries in Massachusetts*. Geoffrey Campbell, operator of the Plymouth Night Tour, introduced me to Michael "Wolf" Pasakarnis who had previously communicated with me in my dreams. He was the young man who was struck by lightning beneath a tree in Plymouth's Burial Hill on September 8, 2010. Oddly, my encounter with the scissors happened on the anniversary of Wolf's tragic death. So, it's possible that he was checking in.

After mysteriously bumping into Wolf's mother, Beth, while touring Burial Hill and learning more about his undying spirit, I decided to dedicate this book to him. Thank you, Wolf.

Special thanks to Joni Mayhan, author of *Signs of Spirits,* for penning the chapter on the Riverside Cemetery and crafting an honorable mention list of haunted burial grounds in a chapter called *Cemetery Dangers*. Mayhan's wisdom and hands-on experience at several of New England's most haunted locations is featured throughout the manuscript. Photographers Frank C. Grace and Jason Baker deserve a supernatural slap on the back for capturing the eerie aesthetic of the main haunts in the *13 Most Haunted* countdown. Major thanks to the handful of paranormal investigators and researchers who helped make *13 Most Haunted Cemeteries in Massachusetts* a reality, including *Destination America's* Jack Kenna, who penned the book's foreword, Essex County Ghost Project's Thomas Spitalere, *New England Folklore's* Peter Muise, James Annitto, Russ Stiver, Michael Baker from Para-Boston, investigator Rachel Hoffman from Paranormal Xpeditions and Adam Berry from TLC's *Kindred Spirits* and Scott Porter and Tim Weisberg from Destination America's *Haunted Towns*. The team from the syndicated TV show *What's New? Massachusetts* and Somerville Media Center

(SMC), including my co-host Sharon Fillyaw and director Mike Cultrera, deserve an old-school high five for helping me with the TV show component of the project. Thanks to my mother, Deborah Hughes Dutcher, for being there when I need her most and my friends for their continued support.

FOREWORD

"Is it possible that your soul continues to exist long after your physical body fails you?"

—Jack Kenna, author of "Paranormal Research"

I've never been a huge believer in cemeteries being haunted. Think about it. After you pass on, do you really want to hang around your gravesite? I mean, yes, I might want to stop by just to check it out, but more likely I would do this during my funeral when my family was there so I could provide emotional support for them, assuming we can still do that sort of thing after we die.

My point is why would a spirit want to haunt a cemetery? If they do linger in burial grounds, then what type of spirit haunts them and what kind of cemeteries are most likely to be haunted? Then there's the ultimate question for paranormal investigators, why would we want to investigate a cemetery?

It was during a S.P.I.R.I.T.S. of New England's investigation at a residential case in Springfield, Massachusetts back in 2010 that I found, at least in this one instance, the answers to these four questions. With the case in mind, let me provide you with my own insights into haunted cemeteries and at least one possible answer to each of the four questions. Of course, it's mainly common sense, at least as much as one can have when it comes to the realm of the paranormal.

Why would a spirit want to haunt a cemetery? It's a valid question, and as I said before I originally didn't believe that one would. During our Bay Path Cemetery case in Springfield, the reason became obvious to me at the surprisingly haunted location on Blunt Park Road. Driving by it, one would not even know it's a cemetery if it wasn't marked by an old wooden sign. It's a small cemetery, less than half the size of a football field and enclosed by a simple chain-link fence. As a matter of fact, one might think it was the yard of a neighboring house if there wasn't a sign. There are no headstones or visible markers. There's one monument stone surrounded by two rose bushes, and a flag pole that's mounted in the earth behind the monument stone. The following is inscribed on the memorial: *"Bay Path Cemetery, 1873-1954. Blessed are the poor in spirit for theirs is the kingdom of heaven."*

Standing inside the plot and reading the memorial, I had no idea that in the small space there were over one-thousand souls buried beneath my feet. Bay Path is an old cemetery for paupers. Those buried there are the unwanted, poor and insane. They were the forgotten souls of the Springfield community.

From 1873-1954, the city did what they could to care for these people in the old almshouse or "poor house" while they were alive. And then they did what they could to provide the poor souls with some kind of final resting place. Unfortunately, the location was all but forgotten after 1954 by the city until a local couple brought it to the attention of the state of Massachusetts in 1980.

The fence, monument, rose bushes and flagpole are from the couple's efforts to push the state and city to do something for the forgotten souls buried there. If this doesn't seem to answer the question as to why would a spirit haunt it, let me put it in plain terms: The spirits of these souls are literally lost. They were buried without any formal services nor were they provided a proper gravestone except for a small round brass marker with a number on it. And yes, these numbers correspond to a name in a ledger in the city clerks' archives.

I believe many of these souls are not at rest, and they wander not only the cemetery but also the surrounding area which was once the old almshouse grounds.

They were drawn to the residence we were investigating. Why? First, the client had been a nurse working at a local hospital which stands at the exact location of the old almshouse. Second, the client was himself suffering from a terminal illness. We believe that these spirits recognized our client from his work at the hospital and they were drawn to him because of his own illness. He also lived less than five-hundred yards from Bay Path Cemetery.

What type of spirits haunt cemeteries? In the case of Bay Path, I believe they are lost souls or the forgotten of society that didn't receive any or very limited religious rights when they were interred. The ground on which they are buried is also not consecrated which I believe leaves the land's energy in a natural state of turmoil. Most importantly, I believe the manner in which the dead bodies were handled in this cemetery attributed to their spirits not being able to find peace. Many were redisturbed over the years in order to make room for others.

What type of cemeteries are most likely to be haunted? Based on my own experiences with Bay Path Cemetery, as well as a few others I have come across since that case, the most likely cemeteries to be haunted are those that are neglected, forgotten and have unconsecrated ground. Active burial grounds usually contain society's "disposable" or "undesirable" people.

I'm not ruling out the possibility that other cemeteries can't be haunted. Even the best and most beautiful of cemeteries contain the poor and forgotten. Some host the skeletal remains of people who were accused of things they never did, or even the souls of the accusers who can't find peace in the afterlife because of what they did to others. For example, unrest is a recurring theme with some of the cemeteries relating to the Salem witch trials.

Why would I want to investigate a cemetery? Normally I wouldn't want to investigate a graveyard. I personally see no purpose in it unless I'm trying to find answers. There are those investigators, like my good friend Sam Baltrusis, who investigate cemeteries in an attempt to understand the history and the stories associated with the individuals behind the hauntings.

Whether he wants to admit it or not, Sam is an empath and sensitive to the paranormal like myself. These abilities allow him to make a unique connection with the spirit world in order to gain information and insights that would otherwise be difficult or impossible to obtain through pure physical research of historical documents. While most people believe any information obtained by the means of supposed "psychic abilities" is purely subjective or even nonsense, I would tell those people to stay open to the possibility. Often when paranormal researchers compare the findings with data collected from investigations such as the electronic voice phenomena (EVPs), video evidence and empathic experiences, we then find a direct correlation to the documented history.

When reading this book, keep an open mind to the possibility of life after death. Is it possible that your soul continues to exist long after your physical body fails you? Consider the stories discussed in *13 Most Haunted Cemeteries in Massachusetts* and why these hauntings may likely be occurring.

Most importantly, consider the state of your soul and ask yourself, "Will I be ready to move on when my time comes?" Some of the spirits featured in this book remain earthbound, haunted by the deeds of their lives. Others stick around because they believed they were wronged in life and couldn't rest until they found justice.

Jack Kenna, a a paranormal investigator and the author of *Paranormal Research: A Comprehensive Guide to Building a Strong Team*. He has been featured on several TV shows on Destination America including *Haunted Case Files* and *Paranormal Survivor*.

INTRODUCTION

"It's my belief that the paranormal activity at New England's haunted cemeteries are psychic remnants of the unjust killings and unmarked graves leftover from centuries of tainted dirt from the Bay State's dark past."
    —Sam Baltrusis, author of *"13 Most Haunted Cemeteries in Massachusetts"*

If one bases my ghost-hunting persona purely on the three paranormal-themed TV shows I've appeared on over the years, I have an odd fixation for the most haunted cemeteries in Massachusetts. As the author of nine historical-based ghost books, I've spent many sleepless nights frolicking among the headstones in search of the skeletal secrets buried beneath the Bay State's blood-stained soil.

Apparently, I have a thing for historic cemeteries. And, yes, it's true. I tend to gravitate toward graveyards.

When it comes to paranormal investigations in cemeteries, demonologist James Annitto told me that they're perfect for beginners looking to learn the tricks of trade. He said New England's historic burial grounds may have "lots of contamination, but that's what makes you a great investigator and how you learn," he told me, adding that outdoor locations are difficult for the most experienced paranormal investigators because of false-positive readings on equipment because of noise, temperature fluctuations and wind. "It gives you the ability to decipher what's contamination and what is plausible paranormal activity. I started out doing graveyards and cemeteries. You would just need to call and get permission."

As far as my most profound experiences with spirits in old burial grounds, my "ghostdar" initially led me to a small, two-block path in downtown Salem called Charter Street. Crafted in 1768, this well-trafficked pathway once connected the town wharf and the present-day Market Street. It also boasts the second-oldest graveyard in the country and arguably Salem's most visited.

The Burying Point, also known as the Charter Street Cemetery, is a familiar location for pop culture representations of the "Witch City," serving as a backdrop for paranormal-themed shows like *Ghost Adventures* and *Ghost Hunters*. It's also where I filmed two national TV shows in 2017, Destination America's *Haunted Towns* and the Travel Channel's *Haunted USA*.

When it comes to Salem's historic cemeteries, it seems that they're chock-full of paranormal activity. Why? Tina Storer, former paranormal investigator known for her work with Paranormal Xpeditions, said the 1692 witch trials hysteria left a psychic imprint of sorts on the area. "Something as tragic as the witch trials can definitely attract activity, from the mere disrespect that occurred to the bodies after death," she said, adding that the lack of a proper burial for the nineteen innocent victims who were hanged at Proctor's Ledge and one, Giles Corey, who was pressed to death, could serve as a spirit magnet.

However, Salem's creepy burial grounds aren't necessarily the North Shore's most active places. "It's easy to think of cemeteries as being haunted. It's a place associated with death. But I don't think it's any different than any other location personally," Storer continued. "Spirits are everywhere, and cemeteries are just pinpointing a location to their place of rest."

The Samuel Pickman House, located on the corner of Charter and Liberty Streets, is said to be home to an evil entity connected to a horrific murder committed centuries ago. *Photo by Frank C. Grace.*

Michael Baker, a scientific-minded paranormal investigator with Para-Boston, echoes Storer's belief. The researcher conducted an exhaustive study for his New England Center for the Advancement of Paranormal Science (NECAPS) on points of geothermal and electromagnetic energy in New England in an attempt to predict active locations. According to Baker, patterns did emerge including a preponderance of paranormal incidents along fault lines, railroad tracks and areas where there are higher reports of UFO sightings. However, the study concluded that graveyards were oddly void of activity. "We left no stone unturned, even cemeteries." Baker said. "We found that there is no correlation to hauntings and cemeteries which goes against what a lot of people believe."

Haunted or not, Salem's cemeteries continue to be a hot spot for ghost lore enthusiasts and amateur investigators. In fact, Sarah-Frankie Carter, a Salem-based tour guide and featured subject on the History Channel 2's documentary highlighting the city's haunted history, said she stays away from the Howard Street Cemetery after having an alleged encounter with the ominous ghost of Giles Corey. However, Carter said Howard Street's cemetery isn't the North Shore's most haunted. According to Carter, the most active graveyard is in nearby

Peabody. "There's one spirit that resides at the St. Mary's Cemetery on Route 114," Carter claimed. "I've seen a full-bodied apparition of a woman there three different times. She's pretty reliable. I've seen her almost every time I've gone in there."

According to multiple reports, visitors at St. Mary's Cemetery in Peabody have spotted "faint white lights" that move around and experienced a foreboding sensation that one should quickly leave. There are also several EVPs of both male and female voices. Carter claimed she had several close encounters of the paranormal kind with one of St. Mary's resident lady specters.

The first time was after midnight several years ago, when Carter and her two friends spotted what looked like a plastic bag stuck in a tree. After a second glance, she said it was a female spirit wearing a nightgown. "She crawled out of the tree and started running right at us," Carter emotively recalled. "It was so dark, but we could see her. She was glowing. We were terrified, and we ran out." Carter's second visit was with a psychic friend who also spotted the female phantom "The spirit was in her twenties, and she died young. I haven't gone back to find her gravestone, but she hangs around a certain spot in the cemetery." The third time that Carter encountered the female specter was with a friend who didn't believe in ghosts. "He looks up and sees her," Carter recalled with a laugh. "He quickly ran out and refused to go back."

Author Nathaniel Hawthorne met his wife, Sophia Peabody Hawthorne, at a lavish dinner party at the Grimshawe House, 53 Charter Street, next to the Old Burying Point. *Photo by Frank C. Grace.*

Based on my nationally televised stint as Boston's paranormal expert on the Biography Channel's *Haunted Encounters* in 2012, cemeteries are the perfect backdrop for on-location TV shoots. The interview, which was shot in front of the Central Burying Ground and facing what I called Boston's "haunted corridor" near the corner of Boylston and Tremont Streets, explored the residual energy, or psychic imprint, left over from the 1897 gas-line explosion. The area surrounding the country's oldest underground subway station, the Boylston Street "T" stop, has been a hot spot of alleged paranormal activity. Why? Beneath what was a dead man dumping ground for British soldiers killed during the Revolutionary War is a series of vacated "ghost tunnels" that cuts through what was, in essence, a mass grave site.

In early 1895, the human remains of hundreds of dead bodies were uncovered during the excavation of the nation's first underground trolley station, now the Boylston Green Line stop. A mob scene of "curiosity seekers" lined up along the Boylston Street corner of the Common "looking at the upturning of the soil," according to the April 18, 1895 edition of the *Boston Daily Globe*. The report continued, saying that "a large number of human bones and skulls are being unearthed as the digging on the Boylston Street mall" progressed. Thrill-seeking spectators were horrified by the sights and smells emanating from the site and were forced to move by early May.

And that was just the first round of skeletons in the Boston Common's collective closet. As the excavation continued, officials uncovered the remains of hundreds—some historians estimated between 900 and 1,100 bodies—buried in shallow graves beneath the Boylston Street mall.

There's a generic gravestone at the Central Burying Ground honoring the hundreds of bodies uncovered during the trolley station excavation. The marker reads: "Here were re-interred the remains of persons found under the Boylston Street mall during the digging of the subway 1895."

While researching a Halloween-themed story for a local magazine, I started spending hours in the Boston Common. I've always felt a strong magnetic pull to the site of the Great Elm, also known as the hanging tree. I also had an inexplicable interest in the Central Burying Ground, and one night while walking by the old cemetery, I noticed a young female figure wearing what looked like a hospital gown and standing by a tree. I looked back and she was gone. At this point, I didn't know about the Matthew Rutger legend dating back to the 1970s. Like me, he saw a ghost at the old cemetery, and I remember shivering in the beauty and the madness of the moment. Somehow, I felt her pain.

Adam Berry, from the television show *Kindred Spirits*, told me that he was drawn to the Central Burying Ground in 2003 while studying at the Boston Conservatory. "I thought that I had a ghost in my dorm room at the Conservatory during my junior year," Berry said, adding that he felt a presence physically hold him down, a phenomenon known as sleep paralysis. "I was freaked out and thought there was something in my room. My mother told me to take some dirt from the front of my dorm and throw it in the cemetery. We did and dumped the dirt in the old cemetery near Emerson [Central Burying Ground] to get rid of the spirit," he remarked.

Based on his experience in 2004, Berry said that he would put Boston's Central Burying Ground at the top of his most-haunted list. "That cemetery definitely has an appeal, like all old cemeteries. There's so much history there in that space, and walking through you get a sense that each gravestone is talking to you. The older the cemetery, the more intimidating. I would definitely put that cemetery at the top of my list."

It's my belief that the paranormal activity at New England's haunted cemeteries are psychic remnants of the unjust killings and unmarked graves leftover from centuries of tainted dirt from the Bay State's dark past.

Of course, cemeteries are not all doom and gloom. People say "rest in peace" when a loved one passes for a reason.

Brian Gerraughty, a regular on my "Graveyard Getaway" jaunts to allegedly haunted cemeteries, told me that it makes sense that burial grounds are more paranormally active. "It has been my personal experience and also from discussions with others in the field that many spirits visit their resting places occasionally to connect with those left behind," Gerraughty said. "It would be a logical place for two planes of existence to overlap."

In addition to paying respect to the dead, burial grounds also served as a park-and-recreation area during the late nineteenth century In fact, it was common during the Victorian era for Americans to picnic in graveyards.

Yes, people would actually "dig in" at cemeteries … and we're not talking about grave diggers.

"It wasn't just apple-munching alongside the winding avenues of graveyards," wrote Jonathan Kendall in *Atlas Obscura*. "Since many municipalities still lacked proper recreational areas, many people had full-blown picnics in their local cemeteries. The tombstone-laden fields were the closest things, then, to modern-day public parks."

As my psychic-medium friend Kristen Cappucci jokingly told me, cemeteries are almost like postmortem party spots for spirits. Wanna dance with the dead? I've assembled a motley crew of the thirteen most haunted cemeteries in Massachusetts.

There are multiple reports of a teen spirit dressed in a hospital gown in Boston's Central Burying Ground. *Photo by Frank C. Grace.*

SKELETAL SECRETS: KELLY DANIELL

"If his family did take his body down from the scaffolding, it's most likely he would be buried on his property."
—Kelly Daniell, Peabody Historical Society

Kelly Daniell, archivist with the Peabody Historical Society, is on a mission to find out where Salem Village's enigmatic son, John Proctor, was buried. Leaving no gravestone unturned, she may have uncovered a few skeletons, both figuratively and literally, in Proctor's seventeenth-century closet.

"When people think of John Proctor they automatically think of Arthur Miller's play *The Crucible*," Daniell said from her office in the historic Osborn-Salata House in Peabody. "They think of Daniel Day-Lewis with his sexy hair and bad teeth," she said with a laugh.

For those who missed the big-screen version of Arthur Miller's *The Crucible*, Proctor was venerated in the iconic play turned movie as the town martyr wrongly hanged for witchcraft in 1692. In the film adaptation, the yeoman farmer and tavern keeper was portrayed by the three-time Oscar winner..

"Daniel Day-Lewis was in his thirties when that movie was made," the archivist said. "At the time of the witch trials, John Proctor was sixty and he had eleven children from three wives. At this point, Proctor had a hard life and he had a lot of children. His third wife, Elizabeth, was about twenty years younger than him."

According to Daniell, there is no way Proctor had an affair with witch-trials accuser, Abigail Williams, portrayed by Winona Ryder in the movie. In 1692, Proctor was an elderly man and Williams was only eleven or twelve.

"There is no historical evidence that they had any type of relationship," Daniell confirmed. "They would have known of each other but they didn't live near each other. He was in Peabody and she lived in what is now the Danvers area. It was a small community so they probably did know about each other, but that's about it."

Daniell believes Arthur Miller used Proctor's servant, Mary Warren, as inspiration for the villainous Abigail Williams role, citing a thin piece of evidence that suggested there was a sexual relationship with Proctor and Warren.

"Mary was working in the Proctor household and was one of the primary accusers in the witch trials," said Daniell, also adding that Warren was the oldest among the afflicted girls. "She lived and worked at the tavern run by John and Elizabeth Proctor. When the accusations started flying, Mary Warren became hysterical. Looking at the historical accounts, it sounded like she was having panic attacks. She's also having these visions and claiming that she was getting touched and pinched."

Warren, whose testimony resulted in eight hangings, was sent to Salem Village to appear in front of the Court of Oyer and Terminer in the Rebecca Nurse trial. "When John Proctor found out that she was testifying in Salem Village, he casually chatted with a man in a tavern on his way to get her," Daniell said.

Kelly Daniell is an archivist with the Peabody Historical Society and spearheaded the efforts to uncover John Proctor's gravesite. *Photo courtesy Kelly Daniell.*

According to the testimony of Samuel Sibley, Proctor referred to Warren as his "jade" and planned to bring her home and beat her. While linguists translate "jade" as a derogatory slur toward women, Daniell said it could have been misinterpreted. "There's some discussion that the term 'jade' implied a possible sexual relationship," Daniell explained. "The second piece of evidence is when Mary Warren later testified that she dreamed of John Proctor laying his head on her lap."

Looking at the case with a modern lens, Daniell said Proctor's relationship with Warren could be viewed as domestic violence. "You have a sixty-year-old man in power with a twenty-year-old woman who works for him," she said. "Was it a relationship or was it abuse?"

As far as the myth that Proctor and *The Crucible*'s villain had a sexual affair, Daniell said Arthur Miller may have thought Abigail Williams's living situation made more sense for his allegory on McCarthyism in the 1950s. "Abigail Williams is a bit of a spicier figure because she's living with the Rev. Samuel Parris," the thirty-year-old explained. "So the idea that John Proctor could be having a relationship with a girl that lives in the reverend's household and she's engaging in some type of witchcraft, that's definitely spicier."

But what did Williams and Warren have in common other than they were both afflicted girls? "Abigail Williams and Mary Warren occupied the same amount of power in society at the time," Daniell said, "which was very little."

Unlike Williams, Warren was an accuser who later became one of the accused. "Mary Warren ends up in jail," Daniell continued. "However, she is responsible for a lot of the allegations against John and Elizabeth Proctor. There is something going on with her mentally and her relationship with the Proctors. She definitely doesn't seem to have liked Elizabeth Proctor."

However, Warren's boss wasn't a saint either. "People always try to compare his real-life character to the one they see in the play or movie," she said. "John Proctor in *The Crucible* is a man all about honor and taking care of the women in his life. Based on historical records, he's not a gentle man. It's suggested that he is a very tall, looming and intimidating person. I'm assuming he would be an intimidating figure to Mary Warren and other people in his life."

Another misconception that Daniell dispelled during her stint with the Peabody Historical Society is that Proctor was a wealthy landowner. Oddly, Proctor was a renter.

"We were surprised to find out he was renting that property," Daniell told me. "Proctor rented his house from a man named Emanuel Downing. He was also farming the land known as Downing Farm and ran a tavern. He got a tavern license in 1666 to give food and drink to travelers on Ipswich Road. As a tavern owner, he was doing very well by the time of the witch trials."

In fact, Proctor had been successfully running his tavern for more than twenty-five years before he and his wife were accused of witchcraft. One theory is that Proctor was so successful that it fueled a rivalry with the nearby Ingersoll's Tavern. However, Daniell said it's unlikely. "Ingersoll's Tavern was here," she said, pointing to present-day Danvers on a historic map. "Proctor was serving people who traveled on Ipswich Road which is here in Peabody. They are too far from each other, in my opinion, to be considered competition."

It was Daniell's passion for maps that led her to her ultimate historic find. In 2017, Daniell was asked to participate in a documentary on the Salem witch trials. Maine-based Lone Wolf Media, which produces documentaries shown on major cable outlets such as The History Channel, The Smithsonian Channel and National Geographic, was interested in Daniell's take on Proctor, specifically what happened to him after he was executed.

During the filming, Daniell may have solved one of the many lingering mysteries involving Proctor. Local lore suggested that his skeletal remains were brought back by relatives, salvaged in the wee hours of the night and given a proper burial after his brutal hanging on August 19, 1692. Based on at least one published report, she intuitively knew his remains were somewhere in present-day Peabody.

But witch way?

Daniell had access to some key historical documents buried within the city's special collections. "In the documentary we go on this journey to all of the sites relating to Proctor," she explained. "Based on documents in our archives, we found out that he was renting the property where he lived. It's kind of wrong for us to call the house on Lowell Street the Proctor House. It's unlikely that he was was buried there because you can't bury a relative on rental property."

However, the historian did find out that the Proctors owned a fifteen-acre plot of land up Lowell Street. "If his family did take his body down from the scaffolding, it's most likely he would be buried on his property," she said. "In the documentary we follow the idea that one of Proctor's adult sons, probably Thorndike, could have taken his body from Gallows Hill and down Proctor's Brook which runs right by his rental property and directly leads to the fifteen acres. There is also oral history that suggests that Proctor was buried on the fifteen acres he owned."

. Daniell's Nancy Drew moment happened while searching online. Her tool of choice? Google Maps.

"This land is oddly untouched," she said, showing me an aerial shot taken from a contemporary online view and juxtaposing it with a historic, hand-drawn map. "Peabody's Veterans Memorial High School is on the property. Based on oral history, he's buried on a corner of land where two walls meet. Oddly, that strip of land where we think he was buried was purchased by the city."

Did they find Proctor's remains? "We didn't do any digging because the land was too rocky," she said, joking that the wooded area is historically known for its after-school parties attracting underage drinkers. "The fact that the land was still there, untouched except for some poison ivy and a few beer cans, is astonishing."

When it comes to the importance of her historical find, Daniell is humble. "We just happened to be the historical society that had the most clues as to where John Proctor might be buried," she told me. "I'm among the new wave of researchers piggybacking off of the work done in the late 1800s and then the 1970s. I'm just picking up the pieces."

Profile of archivist Kelly Daniell is an excerpt from the book *Wicked Salem: Exploring Lingering Lore and Legends* by author Sam Baltrusis.

The bronze statue of Roger Conant, founder of Salem, was unveiled in 1913. *Photo by Sam Baltrusis.*

Chapter 1
HOWARD STREET CEMETERY
Salem
Most Haunted: #1

"People often see an old man go around a tree in there. It seems to be the spirit of Giles Corey."

—*Tim Maguire, Salem Night Tour*

When accused witch and landowner Giles Corey was pressed to death over a two-day period, he allegedly cursed the sheriff and the city. Over the years, his specter has been spotted preceding disasters in Salem, including the fire that destroyed most of the downtown area in June 1914.

Corey supposedly unleashed his curse at the Howard Street Cemetery next to present-day Bit Bar Salem which has a past life as a burger joint called A&B Salem. "The rumor is if you see him, there is sudden death or heart-related death issues," said former tenant Amy Butler. "I had a witch of Salem come up to the door and tell me if I see him, it's over."

Butler, co-owner of A&B Salem, said she was wary looking out at the Howard Street Cemetery. "They say Giles appears in the windows of my building," she continued. "I had two women come who said they had an 'out of body' experience at the previous restaurant. They were attached to the table, shaking like crazy. I guess they were mediums, and they said they could feel the spirits in the building."

A&B Salem, which recently relocated to Beverly, moved out the old jail and Bit Bar Salem set up shop in early 2016.

Visitors to Bit Bar Salem's restaurant and arcade can get a ringside seat to the state's most haunted cemetery. Opened next to the old Salem Jail, the spooky graveyard on a hill is the final resting spot for seafarer Benjamin Ropes, who was buried there on August 5, 1801. Cause of death? Ropes was fatally crushed while launching the historic ship *Belisarius*'s top mast. Oddly, a large percentage of those buried in the Howard Street Cemetery had a fate similar to Giles Corey, the only witch-trials victim who suffered the "peine forte et dure" form of execution. Yep, a large percentage of those buried there were accidentally or purposefully crushed.

"We did some research with the city, and we found that a high number of the people buried in the Howard Street Cemetery, around fifteen percent, were crushed to death," explained Tim Maguire, tour owner and historian. "It's so interesting because that was the site where Giles Corey was crushed to death during the witch trials."

The Salem Night Tour owner rattled off a series of bizarre "accidents" of those buried at the Howard Street Cemetery. "For example, the floor of the jail collapsed and killed ten prisoners," he said. "A high number of people buried there were crushed to death because of various accidents."

Maguire was a featured player on the History Channel 2's documentary focusing on a handful of Salem's alleged haunts. The evidence he unveiled on the show, specifically a photo taken at the Howard Street Cemetery, was shocking. The picture looked like a crowd of Puritan-era revelers, gathered in a lynch mob sort of way, around what is believed to be the exact spot where Corey was stripped naked, placed under a wooden board and crushed to death over a two-day period in 1692.

"Someone on my tour took a photo of the cemetery," Maguire said on the History Channel. "By the end of the tour that person came forward to share the photo they took. Definitely not what we were looking at. There seems to be figures of people standing over someone. Most people who feel like they found the spirit of Giles Corey or have seen his apparition, they think it's a reminder of what we have done to him there."

Maguire told me that he rarely gives daytime tours. However, a Christian-based group requested an earlier time slot one day, and they snapped the infamous picture. "In the photo, you see what looks like flames in the background, and you can make out a couple of faces in the photo," he said, convinced he captured something paranormal. "When we were standing there, it was a nice, clear sunny day."

Over the years, Maguire said he's heard of multiple Corey sightings. "People often see an old man go around a tree in there. It seems to be the spirit of Giles Corey," he said, adding that the burial ground's proximity to the Old Salem Jail adds to its negative energy. "What's interesting about the Howard Street Cemetery is that it was built to accommodate inmate atrocities. It was the only coed jail in the country. Women were on one side, men on the other and children in the middle. There was a four-year-old boy who served a two-month sentence for breaking something."

It's common for visitors to report heart palpitations or a sensation of a heavy weight being placed on their upper body, just like the stubborn landowner who had rocks placed on his chest. It's also the norm for Salemites to mention Corey's curse.

"All of the Essex County sheriffs who overlooked that property eventually died of a heart-related ailment," said Maguire. "Robert Cahill (author of *Haunted Happenings* and sheriff who lived to seventy) was a firm believer in the curse. He had a bizarre blood ailment they couldn't diagnose. It's believed that Corey cursed the city and the sheriff in blood…and we have proof."

And if someone sees his apparition? Salem allegedly burns.

"My friend and I were exploring the Howard Street Cemetery," recalled Sarah-Frankie Carter on the History Channel. "There was a very creepy feeling as we got closer and closer to the spot where Giles Corey was actually pressed to death. My friend wiggled through a fence to see if she could get a closer look at the jail, and I heard her scream. She said she saw a man standing at the top of the stairs. We both had a really bad feeling."

Carter echoed the legend that if the "skeleton of Corey's ghost in tattered old clothes" appears, something horrible will happen to the city. "They say if you see Giles Corey, Salem burns. And if he speaks to you, you die," she said, adding that Salem did, in fact, go up in flames after her Corey sighting. "I was listening to my local college radio station, and they said there were fires in Salem. Needless to say, I don't go to that part of Salem anymore, especially at night. I don't think he gives you that many chances."

One of three cemeteries significant to the Salem witch trials, the Howard Street Cemetery is said to be where Giles Corey was taken to be pressed to death. *Photo by Sam Baltrusis.*

Locals believe in Corey's curse. In fact, author Nathaniel Hawthorne claimed that the apparition "of the wizard appears as a precursor to some great calamity impending over the community."

According to several accounts, Corey's spirit was spotted near the Howard Street Cemetery days before the Great Fire of 1914 that completely annihilated two-thirds of the city. Ironically, the inferno began in Gallows Hill, where nineteen innocents were hanged, and the conflagration destroyed one-third of Salem. "Before the Great Fire of 1914, there were almost three hundred accounts of local Salemites who had gone to the sheriff's office and reported this old man in ragged clothes that they tried to help and then who vanished," confirmed Maguire, adding that he doesn't have solid proof of the lore. "They put enough stock into these accounts that the sheriff put deputies around the Howard Street Cemetery. They actually watched that cemetery for six or seven hours and when they had left, the Great Fire happened about a half-hour after."

Apparently, Corey's spirit continues to hold the city of Salem accountable.

As a veteran tour guide in Salem, I've heard all sorts of stories relating to the often overlooked burial ground next to what was the city's old jail.

Plymouth's Burial Hill has a mass grave for the victims of the brigantine General Arnold tragedy. *Photo by Frank C. Grace.*

Chapter 2
BURIAL HILL

Plymouth
Most Haunted: #2

"Burial Hill isn't necessarily haunted by the people buried in the ground, but the people reliving what they did during their lives."
—Darcy H. Lee, *Ghosts of Plymouth, Massachusetts*

Why is "America's Hometown" so haunted? Darcy H. Lee, author of *Ghosts of Plymouth, Massachusetts*, believes the blood-stained events that unfolded in the early seventeenth century has left a psychic imprint on the land surrounding Burial Hill in Plymouth's Town Square.

"When the Pilgrims landed in 1620, there were more than one hundred on board and only fifty survived," Lee told me. "One of the most haunted places is Town Square, which is near the place where the Pilgrims had their first settlement. Just prior to the Pilgrims landing, there was a plague that decimated the Native Americans that lived there. The desperation and fear of the the Native Americans who lived and died there is embedded into the ground."

Based purely on its historical legacy and the harsh conditions that nearly annihilated America's earliest settlers in 1620, Plymouth is one of New England's most haunted cities. Burial Hill, the town's oldest cemetery, is nestled next to First Parish in Plymouth and located across the street from the Church of the Pilgrimage and the 1749 Court House.

The chaos from four centuries ago still lingers in Plymouth's Town Square. It's almost as if the death and destruction has psychically imprinted itself on the location.

Lee believes there's a Native American spirit guarding Burial Hill near the Cushman Monument. "Legend has it that there is a spot on Burial Hill on top of the staircase by a huge tree," Lee wrote in *Ghosts of Plymouth, Massachusetts*. "The tree has a peculiar feature. It has roots that look like hands. Some say a Native American guardian sits and watches over people at that tree. If a visitor to Burial Hill does anything unacceptable or inappropriate, the guardian spirit will let them know in a terrifying fashion."

Luckily, the Native American sentinel spirit likes me. However, I had a not-so-friendly encounter in early 2018 with a spirit known as "Crazy Mary." She paces back and forth near the cemetery's stairs facing Town Square. When I approached Burial Hill, she lunged at me and I quickly ran down the stairs and back to my room at the John Carver Inn. "She likes to scare people," said Geoffrey Campbell when I told him about my face-to-face encounter with the aggressive female spirit. "She's very sad because people misunderstand her," he told me. "She does scare people off depending on their sensitivities. I had one woman on my tour who walked up the stairs and came running back down the hill. She said that something came after her."

Mary isn't necessarily mentally ill. But, she seems to get a kick out of chasing clairvoyants out of the burial ground.

Campbell, a veteran guide and operator of the Plymouth Night Tour, guided me through the extremely haunted cemetery which is home to several ghosts including scary Mary, a Native American sentinel spirit, a Victorian-era couple and possibly a cryptid known as a Pukwudgie.

Never heard of this mythical creature associated with Plymouth's Wampanoag tribe? It's a little trickster that boasts large ears, fingers and nose. Based on reports including a mention in Henry Wadsworth Longfellow's epic poem "The Song of Hiawatha," the human-shaped gremlin has smooth, grey skin.

Campbell told me that he's seen Burial Hill's Pukwudgies in action. "I was giving a tour a few years ago and we saw three of them dancing around," Campbell insisted. "People were trying to take pictures but it didn't pick up." One tour guide, Vicki Noel Harrington, was in a picture taken outside of the John Carver Inn next to Burial Hill. According to people who have seen the photo, the image looks like a demon peeking over her shoulder.

Campbell believes the "demon" seen in the picture with Harrington is actually a Pukwudgie. "They tend to hide by the mass grave for the soldiers from the brigantine *General Arnold*," he said, pointing to an area in the back next to a copse of trees. "We've had several sightings from the path leading to the monument."

Of course, the story about the ill-fated mariners of the *General Arnold* is legendary in Plymouth. During a Christmas Eve blizzard in 1778, seventy-two men literally froze to death after the vessel and its crew, led by Captain James Magee, was stranded on a sandbar in Plymouth Harbor.

"Captain Magee told them to put rum in their shoes to ward off frostbite, but many drank it instead, dying quickly thereafter, their bodies frozen where they sat or stood," wrote Emily Wilcox in *Wicked Local Plymouth* in 2007. "Seamen huddled together against the blinding snow, whistling winds and crashing waves. Some tried to wrap the heavy, canvas sail around themselves to no avail. They shrieked prayers to God and screamed for help from their fellow man. But the *General Arnold* was beyond help."

Campbell said that when the men were retrieved in Plymouth Harbor many of them were frozen in grotesque shapes, some clutching each other in a horrific death grip while others were stacked on top of each other to block the treacherous nor'easter storm.

The bodies of more than seventy frozen soldiers were kept in the 1749 Court House before being buried in a mass grave located in the rear of the cemetery. "The courthouse basically served as a temporary morgue," Campbell said. "I've heard that the courthouse has a residual haunting associated with the tragedy." At the 1749 Court House in Town Square, people have heard phantom footsteps and what sounded like ice melting.

According to several reports, the captain of the brigantine, James Magee, has been spotted in the cemetery, paying postmortem respect to his fallen crew. Darcy H. Lee, author of *Ghosts of Plymouth, Massachusetts*, confirmed the rumors. "We do know that Captain James McGee visited their gravesite and his is a residual haunting in Burial Hill as well," she told me. "It's that imprint of what they were doing in life that remains."

Like Lee, Campbell believes that the spirits haunting Burial Hill are just visiting. "When people see apparitions specifically in this cemetery, they are not usually people who were buried here," Campbell confirmed. "I find that the apparitions are usually here to visit someone buried in the cemetery. I also believe there's a portal in Burial Hill and spirits are able to come through, visit their loved ones and then return back where they came from."

Lee said that one haunting associated with Burial Hill involves a Victorian-era couple who visited the gravestone of their two-year-old daughter, Ida Elizabeth Spear. "Burial Hill isn't necessarily haunted by the people buried in the ground, but the people reliving what they did during their lives," Lee said. "There are reports of a Victorian couple who are visiting the grave of their young daughter who passed away. Their grief and sadness of those visits remain as a residual haunting in Burial Hill. People spot them walking up and down the pathways of the cemetery."

Burial Hill, established in the 1600s, is the burial site of several Pilgrims and the founding settlers of Plymouth. *Photo by Frank C. Grace.*

Of course, this theory applies to a recent tragedy that mysteriously happened on September 8, 2010. Michael "Wolf" Pasakarnis, a Plymouth-based poet and artist, was freakishly struck by lightning on his way home from Blue Blinds Bakery on North Street. Many believe that the twenty-nine-year-old man, known for his piercing eyes and heart of gold, predicted his freakish and untimely death which was posthumously revealed in his cryptic drawings and writings.

In fact, Pasakarnis wrote a poem claiming that "the time has come to allow the light of nature to free my soul" a few days before he passed.

Throughout the Burial Hill tour, Campbell kept finding offerings like a turkey feather and a heart-shaped rock. "This is from my friend Wolf," Campbell confirmed, pointing out that the Jack Skellington hat he was wearing was an homage to Pasakarnis. Apparently, *A Nightmare before Christmas* was Wolf's favorite movie and Campbell led me to the tree where the young man was found dead from electrocution in 2010. There were markings alluding to Wolf's life and love for *Nightmare*, including a "Pumpkin King" smile, etched into the tree. "They originally thought Wolf fell from the tree," Campbell said, recounting Wolf's prophetic last day. "He was with friends at the bakery and then dropped of a heart-shaped rock at the Laughing Moon boutique before heading up to Court Street and finally to Burial Hill."

According to an article by Emily Clark in the November 21, 2010 edition of *Wicked Local*, Wolf left an indelible impact on Plymouth's tight-knit community. "He was standing next to a beech tree when the bolt hit him, exploding his iPod and exiting out the heel of boots his father had just bought him, leaving a jagged hole behind," Clark wrote. "His death stunned a community of friends and downtown regulars who had come to rely on his compassion, his daily walks through town and that mysterious other-worldliness that made so many believe in magic and in things happening for a reason."

When Campbell showed me a picture of Wolf, I gasped. He looked so familiar. In fact, I had recurring dreams of what I thought was a young, Native American man encouraging me to come to Plymouth. It was Wolf.

When I said that I have connected with Wolf's spirit in my dreams, Campbell wasn't surprised. It seems that the young man has connected with other mediums in the past. One clairvoyant, Suzanne Giesemann, wrote an entire book called *Wolf's Message* in 2014 about her psychic interactions with his spirit.

As Campbell and I were talking, the mystery surrounded this mysterious man continued. His mother, Beth, was visiting Burial Hill from out of town and overheard our discussion. She walked up and started sharing stories about her son. It was a few days before the anniversary of his death so she was in town to pay respect and commemorate her son.

"It's almost as if he lived between two worlds," Pasakarnis told me. "When he left the bakery, he told his friends that he 'had to go' as if he knew he had to be here at that time. Even the storm was strange. It came out of nowhere and there was only one random lightning strike."

When I mentioned that I wanted to dedicate *13 Most Haunted Cemeteries in Massachusetts* to her son, she said that he would "get a kick out of it," implying that his spirit is still around. Based on the randomness of meeting his mother in Burial Hill, the feathers and heart-shaped rocks dotting our journey and the recurring dreams, I believe his spirit was around us that day.

Campbell, who regularly eulogizes Wolf on his tours, promised to place two roses at Wolf's tree on the anniversary of his death. He also handed Pasakarnis a feather that he found next to the Cushman Monument. "Here's a gift from Wolf," he said. The mother's eyes started to well up with emotion. "He would leave something like this," Pasakarnis said with a smile. "He's always letting us know that he's still here in spirit."

IN HONOR OF
OVER 300
CIVIL WAR
VETERANS
INTERRED IN THESE
HALLOWED GROUNDS
AND ALL OTHER
VETERANS WHO
SERVED THEIR
COUNTRY IN WAR
AND PEACE

#3

Haverhill's Hilldale Cemetery is believed to be haunted by Civil War-era soldiers. *Photo by Sam Baltrusis.*

Chapter 3
HILLDALE CEMETERY

Haverhill
Most Haunted: #3

"I call cemeteries outdoor museums. Every gravestone has a story to tell."
—Thomas Spitalere, Essex County Ghost Project

Based purely on its eerie aesthetic, Hilldale Cemetery in Haverhill should be haunted. It has all of the telltale signs: Civil War-era soldiers buried in a mass grave, desecrated headstones thanks to years of neglect, a series of unmarked plots where Haverhill's paupers were dumped and urban legends involving all sorts of tales of the macabre, including a larger-than-usual tree believed to be used for hangings.

According to my tour guide, Thomas Spitalere, it's been an uphill battle trying to return this historic cemetery to its original glory. "Over there was a portal that we had to close," he said, talking about an area that has an unusually high level of energy that serves as a doorway to another dimension.

Spitalere, president of the cemetery's board of trustees, told me that he's encountered an onslaught of paranormal phenomenon with his group of investigators called Essex County Ghost Project. There's a lady in white who reportedly rushes up to people in the cemetery. According to several psychics, she's mourning the loss of her soldier boyfriend. "She's wearing what looks like an old-school wedding dress," Spitalere said, adding that perhaps the ghostly lady continues to search for her mortally wounded love in the afterlife. "And over there we uncovered shadow figures," he said, pointing to an area near what has been divined as the hanging tree. "Near Soldier's Hill we have a photo of what looks like a head coming out of the ground."

The historian directed me to what he jokingly calls his "office," which happens to be the trunk of his car. He whipped out a binder of research and paranormal photos, including a picture of a soldier's grave and, yes, there appears to be a disembodied head emerging in front of the commemorative marker.

When Spitalere's team researched the backstory of the soldier spirit, they learned that the floating head emerged in front of Henry J. White's gravestone. Spitalere said the man had an illustrious career as a drummer during the Civil War and even taught young soldiers the art of various drum rolls. The syncopated rhythms from the instrument—like "attack now" or "retreat"—reflected military orders during battle because it was difficult for the officers to understand verbal commands amidst the noise and chaos of combat.

However, not all of the spirits in Hilldale Cemetery are positive manifestations.

"We also have another lady who plays hide and seek with us," Spitalere said, adding that the entity wears Victorian-era garb and was more nefarious compared to the other female spirit in the wedding dress. "Over on what we call 'hangman's hill' we had a few nasty things up there."

If Spitalere's account sounds like a cavalcade of fearsome phantoms pulled from the imagination of author H.P. Lovecraft, then it should be no surprise that the horror writer's friend and his first publisher is actually buried at Hilldale Cemetery. Yep, Charles W. "Tryout" Smith was interred down a path leading to what looks like a crevasse caused by the burial ground's glacial formations. A commemorative headstone honoring Smith's legacy in Haverhill was dedicated in September 2018.

For Spitalere, Hilldale is a historical goldmine of information from the Civil War era to the 1980s. Hilldale Cemetery was founded in 1859 and it's a garden-style burial ground with naturally steep hills caused by glaciers. "I call cemeteries outdoor museums," he told me. "Every gravestone has a story to tell."

In 2008, Spitalere was asked by Essex Heritage to catalog old cemeteries and he eventually was tapped to be the volunteer director of the privately owned Hilldale. Apparently, all of the previous trustees resigned. He said that the burial ground's historical significance is unparalleled, rattling off the shockingly large of amount of skeletal remains in the cemetery that includes at least four hundred Civil War veterans and countless pauper graves.

"There's around 4,820," he told WHAV radio in May 2017. "That's what we have in the book, but we have now located names on stones that aren't in the book. So, once this project is done—the cleaning—we're going to go stone to stone, row to row and recatalog the cemetery."

Five years ago, the cemetery made headlines and not in a good way. Locals started to complain about its condition and Spitalere had to literally explain the hurdles he faced to Haverhill's mayor. In addition to maintaining the yard, he had to combat severe vandalism "including several fires that were intentionally set, damaged gravestones, fence posts that were spray-painted, toppled headstones and trespassing by riders of dirt bikes and other recreational vehicles," reported an article in *The Eagle-Tribune* on August 13, 2013.

Since taking over, Spitalere said at least fifty percent of the gravestones at Hilldale Cemetery have been reclaimed. He also explained that the cemetery was comprised of at least twenty acres in the nineteenth century and is the result of a "terminal moraine," or a geological formation consisting of debris pushed forward by a glacier. The aesthetic is a truly unique landscape consisting of peaks and valleys and what is known as a "kame," or a moundlike hill of sand and gravel.

Caitlyn Pellerin, an empath and Spitalere's fiancée, talked about the spirits she's connected with at the burial ground. She's also channeled a few spirits during investigations including two not-so-nice children entities near the potter's field which is a dead man's dumping ground for paupers.

"Two of them are kids and two of them are not," the Essex County Ghost Project co-founder said, referencing the possibility of an entity manifesting as a child with at least two encounters she's had at Hilldale.

Both Pellerin and Spitalere said the burial ground "hasn't been investigated to death" and is a fairly untapped location for paranormal investigators. However, Spitalere warned that the grounds are private and ghost hunters need permission to access what he believes is the most haunted cemetery in Massachusetts.

He also believes that the large percentage of unkempt and desecrated graves continues to leave a few spirits in unhinged in the afterlife. "I had one team member spot a shadow figure wearing a sailor's hat over there," he said, pointing to one of the rolling hills. "When they went over to investigate, they lifted up the gravestone and put it back in place. We haven't seen that particular shadow figure since that episode."

Spitalere told me that his sensitivity to the paranormal has heightened during his tenure at Hilldale Cemetery. "I've channeled a World War II soldier and I said stuff I will not repeat," he told me. "I also connected with a spirit of a soldier who had his leg blown off by a canon."

When asked why a cemetery would be haunted, Spitalere gave a simple answer to a complex question. "Some spirits just don't want to leave the cemetery," he said. "Why do objects get haunted? Some people just don't know how to let go."

Mary Corey, the second wife of witch-trials victim Giles Corey, is buried in Salem's Old Burying Point. *Photo by Frank C. Grace.*

Chapter 4
OLD BURYING POINT
Salem
Most Haunted: #4

"I actually looked up and saw somebody looking down at me. It was a woman."
—Old Burying Point account from eyewitness at neighboring restaurant

History and mystery oozes from the oldest burial ground in Salem. Also known as the Charter Street Cemetery, the Old Burying Point dates back to 1632, contains the remains of 347 bodies and is one of the oldest cemeteries in the country. In addition to its historical relevance, it was a regular haunt for Salem's native son, Nathaniel Hawthorne, author of the classics *The Scarlet Letter* and *The House of the Seven Gables*.

Buried in the Charter Street Cemetery is Hawthorne's ancestor John Hathorne, a witch-trials judge whose memory haunted him. According to local tours, Hawthorne added the "w" to his name to distance himself from his infamous great-great grandfather. Yes, the writer allegedly abhorred his familial connection to the 1692 witch-trial hysteria. However, we can't prove historically that he added the "w" to his name because of the disdain.

At least eight members of his family were interred there, including his grandparents and two of their daughters. Witch-trial judge Bartholomew Gedney, poet Anne Bradstreet, architect-carver Samuel McIntire and Mayflower passenger Richard More are all buried there. No surprise, but names from the gravestones in the Charter Street Cemetery often appear in Hawthorne's writings. For example, the small gravestone of Hepzibah Packer, who died in 1885, possibly inspired Hawthorne to use the unusual name of Hepzibah in his novel *The House of the Seven Gables*. The same novel also features a character called "John Swinnerton," who shares his name with a real-life Salem doctor buried in the cemetery in the late seventeenth century. The burying ground was also featured in Hawthorne's *Dr. Grimshawe's Secret*.

The Salem-bred author met his wife, Sophia Peabody Hawthorne, at a lavish dinner party at the Peabody family home located at 53 Charter Street, literally next-door to the Old Burying Point. Today it's known as the Grimshawe House. According to lore, Sophia suffered from migraines, and the couple would take midnight strolls in the cemetery. It's believed that the headaches were the result of drugs her father, a Salem dentist, prescribed to her during early childhood to ease her difficulty with teething. The Peabody family lived there between 1835 and 1840 before they moved to Boston.

Today, the Old Burying Point lies adjacent to the Witch Trials Memorial, a small park dedicated in 1992 to honor the memory of the men and women who were executed for witchcraft in 1692. The Grimshawe House, currently being restored, stands as an eerie reminder of Salem's nineteenth-century grandeur.

Nestled next to the highly trafficked Old Burying Point which is also known as the Charter Street Cemetery in Salem, the Samuel Pickman House is now owned by the Peabody Essex Museum. Tour groups pass this historic building and passersby peek through its windows. Several people on my tours believe they've seen a full-bodied apparition of a girl peering from the upper-floor window. Others claim the small Colonial-era structure is home to a demonic entity that manifests in photos taken through the seventeenth-century building's old-school windows.

One ghastly story tells of a husband and wife who lived in the Samuel Pickman House with their seven-year-old daughter. Similar to the demonic infestation in Stephen King's *The Shining*, an evil entity is rumored to have caused the husband to go insane.

According to legend, the man chained his daughter up in the attic, torturing and starving the child. He then tied his wife to a tree outside and killed her by pouring hot wax over her body, leaving her to die a slow, painful death. The possessed man then fled, leaving the dead child in the attic and his murdered-by-wax wife tied to the tree.

People on my walking tours who have taken photos of the house claim it is still inhabited by a demonic force. There are many reports of the ghost of the young girl looking out the attic window at the crowds below.

After doing exhaustive historical research, I found no real proof to suggest that the story of the murder or the supposed demonic infestation at the house is true. However, the building is a surefire hot spot of photographic anomalies, ranging from orbs to a mist that envelops the structure.

As far as paranormal activity, the Charter Street Cemetery is the usual finale for Salem-based ghost tours. Sensitives claim to have an overwhelming feeling of sadness and depression walking through the graveyard and the adjoining Witch Trials Memorial. Some believe the area is tied to a disaster. According to lore, a former inn on Charter Street caught on fire, and a woman and her son escaped while her husband remained inside to put out the blaze. They ran back in for him, but he was dead.

"In the back corner near Murphy's Restaurant and Bar, a woman in a Victorian-era powder blue dress can be seen holding a picnic basket and a young boy in short pants, black shirt and hat is always seen with her," reported the website *Witch City Ghosts*. "Often cameras malfunction but when they do operate properly, the pictures capture bight white streaks of light, paranormal orbs and odd mists."

It's believed that the Victorian-era lady in blue and her son died in the nineteenth-century fire. Apparently, the back corner of the cemetery closest to Murphy's Restaurant is a hot spot for the paranormal. "According to legend, a casket once broke through the wall and fell into the building," added Leslie Rule, writing about the restaurant in *When the Ghosts Scream*. "Employees insist it really happened and point to part of the wall that obviously has been patched. No one knows the identity of the ghosts who wander through the restaurant, but some wonder if they may indeed have escaped from the cemetery next door."

Tim Maguire, co-owner of the Salem Night Tour, said he's heard stories and has seen convincing photos supporting claims that a casket did indeed break through the wall at Roosevelt's Restaurant. "It looked like it was a casket of a small child, possibly a girl," he claimed. "The corner of the cemetery near Murphy's Restaurant is where the Irish Catholics were buried. So, I'm not surprised that it's extremely active."

In addition to orbs and full-bodied apparitions spotted in the cemetery, reports suggest that visitors regularly see a "lady in white." Oddly, she's rarely captured in photos and film. "The cemetery has been the site of the occasional ghostly appearance of a lady in white," wrote Christopher Forest in *North Shore Spirits*. "The ghost itself does not typically appear in person. Rather, it often manifests itself in the form of orbs. It has even appeared as a slight figure in pictures taken at the site."

The lady in white has been spotted in buildings and even in the parking lot.

According to a report from North Andover's *The Eagle-Tribune* in October 2001, the former owner of Roosevelt's Restaurant (the current spot of Murphy's Restaurant and Bar) said he spotted a female apparition when he was working alone in the restaurant at 3 a.m. "I was on the second floor," recalled Henry McGowan. "I actually looked up and saw somebody looking down at me. It was a woman." He did a double take, and the phantom vanished.

So, who is the lady in white? Within the Witch Trials Memorial, one commemorative stone honors witch-trials victims Giles Corey and his wife, Martha. However, his second wife, Mary Corey, was also buried in the Old Burying Point. A small, white gravestone marks her skeletal remains. Historians surmise that stubborn old man was very much in love with his second wife. In fact, she's considered to be the love of his life. Oddly, the lady in white has been seen coming from the general vicinity of her grave marker, and many believe it's her spirit that continues to levitate across the cemetery.

My most profound encounter in Salem several years ago was at Old Burying Point. I spotted a full-bodied apparition of what I believe was Mary Corey coming from what I later learned was her gravestone. She's heading oddly toward the very spot located at the present-day Howard Street Cemetery where the stubborn but determined old man was crushed to death.

Based on encounters, Corey's spirit simmers with a postmortem resentment after being crushed to death under a pile of stones more than three hundred years ago. However, if anything has the power to undo the curse unleashed by Corey, it's surely his enduring love for his second wife. Perhaps Mary's spirit is searching for her tortured husband … and if the two spirits finally meet, the curse will be undone.

Yes, love does exist in the afterlife.

According to a Spider Gates Cemetery urban legend, if you walk around Marmaduke Earle's gravestone ten times and ask he him to speak, he will. *Photo by Frank C. Grace.*

Chapter 5
SPIDER GATES CEMETERY
Leicester
Most Haunted: #5

"I never went back. The place is truly evil."
—Spider Gates Cemetery account from an anonymous source

There are so many myths swirling around the Quaker burial ground, called Friends Cemetery, in Leicester, I didn't know what to expect when I visited. Also known as Spider Gates Cemetery because of the mysterious cobweb-style iron gates welcoming visitors to this allegedly haunted hot spot, its eerie vibe is punctuated by its off-the-beaten path location tucked away near the Worcester airport.

My first impression of this so-called eighth gate to hell? It's nearly impossible to find using a GPS-driven navigation system. Luckily, veteran paranormal photographer Frank C. Grace intuitively knew where to go on Manville Street and my team, including videographer Liz Taegel from the *13 Most Haunted* TV show, meandered down a mosquito-infested path with a yellow gate.

I quickly walked through the marsh to the wrought-iron fence I've heard about for years. It was an oddly foreboding journey back in time. The hanging tree to the left of the wrought-iron fence, where a teen boy is said to have been hanged in the 1980s, served as an eerie sentinel warning visitors of the horrors rumored to have unfolded in this beautifully landscaped Friends Cemetery.

For the record, there is only one gate and not eight. However, this is just the tip of the iceberg regarding the misinformation surrounding this cemetery chock-full of urban legends.

Other Spider Gates stories suggest that there's another cemetery nearby that can only be found once. White ectoplasm supposedly oozes from the ground and the rocks outside of the cemetery wall have runes etched in them. All not true.

But is Spider Gates haunted? Sometimes fact is stranger than fiction.

Taegel, who was lagging behind the team, was filming the trek through the woods and somehow dropped her car keys in the grass. A man, who Taegel described as a skeletal-looking figure accompanied by a female companion came out of nowhere and returned her keys. The gatekeeper's voice was so loud it boomed 50 feet or so to the cemetery. "You dropped your keys ma'am," he said. Taegel recalled later that the gatekeeper enunciated his words with an old-school New England accent. She said his voice sounded like a turn-of-the-century throwback to another era.

The videographer's complexion turned a ghostly white after she interacted with the man and his friend. As soon as Taegel retrieved her keys, the mysterious duo walked into the marshland, which had no clear path, and the videographer said they were gone in a flash.

"The whole interaction was just spooky," mused Taegel in hindsight. "The two came out of nowhere."

Local ghost-lore enthusiast Christine Broderick said she also had a close encounter near the stream where Taegel met the cemetery's gatekeeper. "We went a few years ago to Spider Gates and walked around near the stream," she recalled. "I was alone and my friends were up ahead. I swear it sounded like something was rushing down the woods straight toward me. I thought it was one of my friends trying to scare me. They were running fast so I screamed like a little girl and ran and caught up with my friends."

Broderick continued: "It wasn't them. So they all came back with me and right where I first heard the noise like someone running through the woods a huge tree had fallen and that was definitely not the noise I heard. I thanked the ghosts or whatever because I would be under that tree."

Once entering the so-called eighth gate to hell, visitors are greeted with the cemetery's alleged hanging tree to the left. According to lore, a local teenage boy tied a noose around his neck and somehow jumped from the tree in the 1980s. His spirit is said to follow people around and some claim to have felt the boy tug at their shirt or worse grab unexpected guests around the neck.

Believed to be the eighth gate to hell, Spider Gates Cemetery earned its nickname because of the mysterious cobweb-style iron gates welcoming curiosity seekers. *Photo by Frank C. Grace.*

There are no reported hangings at Friends Cemetery. However, there may actually be a sliver of truth to the tall tale. According to Daniel V. Boudillion, there was a rumored apparent suicide on Manville Road, which is connected to the cemetery by a dirt path. "There was a hanging in the '70s in the area on Manville Street heading toward Paxton Street near the reservoir on the left side," recalled Boudillion on his website. "A mother and daughter were out picking pinecones and found him. I don't remember his name but it was in the paper. He was a local boy and they found him with his hands and feet bound hanging from a tree."

Boudillion also included a picture of what looks like a full-bodied apparition of a boy sitting on the tree. He's greenish in color and seems to be wearing a school uniform. He's called "green boy" and the color is significant in the paranormal realm. It represents nature and the heart. According to paranormal researchers, green symbolizes a spirit that once walked the Earth. So, if it is in fact a ghost, he's earthbound.

Walking past the creepy hanging tree, you can see a spot in the center that people claim was used as a satanic "altar" in black mass rituals and ceremonial sacrifices. The raised area is where the Quaker meetinghouse originally stood. So, the plateau stone posts marking each corner is formerly a foundation. This doesn't rule out the possibility of ritualistic gatherings, especially during the '60s and '70s.

However, the actual location was formerly a spiritual homebase to the Quaker families buried at the Friends Cemetery. The oldest gravestones date back to the 1700s and the most recent burial was in 2000. In other words, it's an active burial ground in more ways than one.

The series of gravestones to the left of the supposed evil altar marks the final resting place of the Earle family. The grave on the far left belongs to Marmaduke Earle, who is the focus of a Spider Gates urban legend. "If you walk around Marmaduke's gravestone ten times at midnight and say 'Marmaduke speak to me,' kneel down and put your head on the gravestone and listen, he would speak to you," Bourdillion's source reported. "I have been there at night and I can say that you could hear groans of some sort but there is a house on Manville Street before the dirt road and the people who lived there are the Grangers. They had cows and when they moo it could sound like groans and moans."

The cemetery is also close to the Worcester airport. While taping our *13 Most Haunted* documentary in 2015, we heard several planes fly overhead and the noise emanated throughout the cemetery.

The nearby airport may be the culprit for another Spider Gates mystery. Visitors report hearing a roar from the wooded area behind the cemetery. Our video team headed into the area and oddly, the batteries to our video camera mysteriously drained. Once we left the spot, the equipment returned to normal.

One woman ventured out to the wooded place where our batteries had drained. "I'll never go back there again," claimed an anonymous source. "I was walking my dog in the area and came upon the cemetery. While I was checking out some of the stones, my dog ran deeper into the cemetery and disappeared near the altar area. I soon heard barking, a yelp and then nothing. When I went looking for him, I found blood everywhere and then nothing. There were no animal tracks around, but there was a horrible smell of sulfur."

The source said Spider Gates is home to a demonic entity. "I never went back," she continued. "The place is truly evil."

Another blogger talked about a horrific experience one night in 1991. "Some stuff happened with my friend," he said. "I chased her into the actual cemetery. Something grabbed me by the arm and threw me down. After that I don't remember but I have the scars on my arm to prove it and they aren't human."

While exploring the wooded area, my team searched for a laid-stone culvert or Shaker-style cave that's believed to be where a young girl was murdered and mutilated. Based on historical research, the story of the female isn't true. However, there was a horrific death involving a six-year-old boy from the Mcauley Nazareth Home for Boys on Mulberry Street. According to reports, he was pummeled to death by a sixteen-year-old classmate and dumped in Lynde Brook, which is less than one mile from Spider Gates.

The photo of the "green boy" taken from the supposed hanging tree fits the description of the murdered six-year-old student. Could the Spider Gates haunting be tied to the Nazareth student and not the unsubstantiated hanging? Yes, it's possible. When it comes to the Friends Cemetery in Leicester, the "green boy" story is only one of a handful of yarns local thrill seekers have weaved.

Central Burying Ground isn't Boston's most visited cemetery, but it's believed to be its most haunted. *Photo by Frank C. Grace*.

Chapter 6
CENTRAL BURYING GROUND
Boston
Most Haunted: #6

"She felt someone or something tap her on the shoulder."
—Jeffrey Doucette, veteran ghost tour guide.

While the nearby Granary Burial Ground earns top billing thanks to its Freedom Trail–friendly names, including Paul Revere, Samuel Adams, John Hancock and even Mother Goose, the Boston Common's lesser-known Central Burying Ground has something that the other graveyards don't: ghosts.

After Boston's Puritan leaders purchased the plot in 1756, the cemetery was used as a final resting spot for foreigners and other paupers who couldn't cough up enough shillings for a proper burial. The graveyard is the resting spot for composer William Billings and artist Gilbert Stuart, who was responsible for painting George Washington's mug on the dollar bill. It is also reportedly the place where the see-through denizens from the Common's spirit realm prefer to hang out.

"Visitors to the graveyard have reported seeing shadowy figures appear nearby, often near trees," wrote Christopher Forest in *Boston's Haunted History*. "The figures disappear or dissolve when people look right at them. Some people have associated the figures with the former hanging victims who met their end on the Boston Common gallows."

Apparently, the cemetery's spirits like to have fun with tourists. "They have been accused of poking people in the back, rattling keys and even brushing up against shoulders. Some people roaming the graveyard have reported being grabbed from behind by an unseen force," he wrote.

Jeffrey Doucette, a veteran tour guide who recently retired, said he was a skeptic until he witnessed a woman have a close encounter with a paranormal force outside the cemetery's gates in 2011. "She felt someone or something tap her on the shoulder," he mused. "She looked annoyed, and I had to assure her that no one was there."

The more notorious haunting at the Central Burying Ground centers on a young female spirit who was described by late great ghost expert Jim McCabe as a teen girl "with long red hair, sunken cheekbones and a mud-splattered gray dress on." On a rainy afternoon in the 1970s, she paid a visit to a dentist named Dr. Matt Rutger, who reportedly experienced "a total deviation from reality as most of us know it." According to Nadler's *Ghosts of Boston Town*, Rutger was checking out the gravestone carvings. He felt a tap on his shoulder and then a violent yank on his collar. No one was there.

As Rutger was bolting from the cemetery, he noticed something out of the corner of his eye. "I saw a young girl standing motionless in the rear corner of the cemetery, staring at me intently," he said. The mischievous spirit then reappeared near the graveyard's gate, almost fifty yards from the initial encounter. Then the unthinkable happened. "He somehow made it by her to Boylston Street, and even though he couldn't see her, he felt her hand slip inside his coat pocket, take out his keys and dangle them in midair before dropping them," McCabe recounted.

Rutger, in an interview with Nadler, said the 1970s-era paranormal encounter has left an indelible mark on his psyche. "One thing is certain, the encounter affected me in very profound ways," he reflected. "As a trained medical professional, I have always seen the world in fairly empirical terms. There's no way something like that cannot completely change how you think about the world."

Doucette, a former ghost guide who now works with Boston Duck Tours, said he was a skeptic for years until he had a few close encounters of the paranormal kind while trudging through his former tour's haunted sites scattered throughout the Boston Common and Beacon Hill. After years giving ghost tours, he's now a full-fledged believer. "I was like, 'What the…? Let's get out of here,'" he said, referring to the red-colored orbs shot in the Central Burying Ground. "It literally freaked me out."

The tour guide, who works in the finance department at a publishing house in Government Center during the day, said he was raised in a superstitious Irish Catholic family. "My grandmother was a tinker, or an Irish gypsy, and she would go to confession and then she would read Tarot cards to make sure she was covering both ends of the spectrum," he joked. "I suspect a little of that tinker mysticism was passed on to me. My mother would always say people would die in threes. When someone passed, we made sure we left the windows open to let the spirits out."

Doucette was an amused skeptic until he gave his first Boston Common tour in 2009. "A kid on the tour shot a photo of me, and there were all of these white orbs near the Great Elm site," he explained. "The last photo really threw me for a loop. It was of me with a green light coming out of my belly, and I was freaked out. Since then, we've had a few orbs here and there, but this year has been out of control. Tonight, I really don't know what happened. Will I sleep? I don't know. But it was something that I've never experienced before."

Doucette said he reached out to a psychic who told him that the green light emanating from his torso was an indication that the spirits in the Boston Common liked the way he told their stories. "At the hanging elm, many of the people who were hanged there were done so unjustifiably by the Puritans for crimes they didn't commit. If anyone disagreed with the status quo at that time, they were executed. Boston was founded by Puritans, and it was either their way or the highway … or the hangman's noose. Even in the modern age, if you disagree with authority, there's the chance that you can be shamed. In my opinion, many of those hanged in the Boston Common were victims of freedom of speech and died at the hands of oppressive authority figures. So when I said on the tour that many of the people hanged at the Great Elm site died innocently, I felt like I was giving them a voice."

Doucette continued, "I've always been respectful of the spirits in the Boston Common. They've never bothered me at home, and I never had an issue with a haunting. But when I did the tours, they did come out. I was a strong advocate for those who were disenfranchised and oppressed, especially women, and they always responded to the stories that I told on the tour."

As far as historical figures are concerned, Doucette said he was drawn to people like Ann "Goody" Glover, who was hanged for allegedly practicing witchcraft on November 16, 1688. Glover, a self-sufficient, strong-willed Irishwoman who spoke fluent Gaelic, lived in the North End, where she washed laundry for John Goodwin and his family. After a spirited spat in her native Gaelic tongue with Goodwin's 13-year-old daughter, Martha, Glover was accused of bewitching the four children in the household and was sent to prison for practicing the dark arts. While Glover was exonerated of her crimes in 1988 and dubbed a "Catholic martyr" three hundred years after her execution, Doucette said he's compelled to tell her story.

However, he's not convinced that Glover's spirit is haunting the Boston Common. "People want a big name to associate with the hauntings in the Common, but I seriously don't think that's the case," adding that "it makes for good storytelling."

Pierce Tomb in Newburyport's Old Hill Burying Ground has been desecrated more than once. *Photo by Sam Baltrusis.*

Chapter 7
OLD HILL BURYING GROUND
Newburyport
Most Haunted: #7

"Our group got some pretty solid responses on the spirit box from the ghost of a young boy who was reported to have drowned in a well."
——Old Hill Burying Ground account from Brian Gerraughty

Newburyport's Old Hill Burying Ground has a few tales from the crypt that continue to haunt this sleepy North Shore enclave. The spirits are in a state of unrest because of a recurring desecration that appears to repeat itself every twenty years.

The haunted hotspot is Pierce Tomb and it's located at the top of the hill. Good luck trying to check it out. Based on a recent visit during an August rainstorm, I had a helluva time trying to get close to the allegedly haunted tomb. In fact, I slipped down the hill several times and literally had to crawl on my knees to stop from rolling over the historic gravestones.

Mission accomplished. Well, kinda sorta. I had a few bumps and bruises from the "rolling stone" incident.

Based on local legend and actual reported fact, Pierce Tomb was broken into by ten teenagers in February 1985. The boys removed the skeletal remains from the coffins and poured alcohol into the mouths of these mummified corpses. The teens set up a clubhouse in the tomb for about three weeks and performed macabre rituals with the dead bodies. There is one woman and six men interred in the Pierce family tomb, including a drowning victim and a Civil War veteran. The first interment was in 1838.

The cemetery's caretaker uncovered the desecration more thirty years ago and notified local authorities. The corpses were returned to their original coffins. However, no one stepped forward to take responsibility for the heinous disrespect of the dead. In an attempt to finger the perpetrators, the local newspaper published an article about the vandalism and claimed that three of the corpses in the tomb died from a contagious disease like tuberculosis. The article in the *Newburyport News* reported that the boys who infiltrated the Pierce Tomb were in danger. After hearing the fake news, the troublemakers turned themselves in to local authorities.

While the vandals were not in danger, the story raised a few eyebrows within the community after locals remembered that a similar desecration happened in the tomb in the early 1900s. It also happened in 2005.

Is there something more sinister at work luring these young men to mess with the skeletal remains within the Pierce Tomb every twenty years?

"I can't help but notice the strange repeat abnormality that surrounds the Pierce Tomb," wrote Daniel V. Boudillion on his blog in 2005. "Teenage boys breaking into the tomb and playing with corpses, and at regular twenty year generational intervals? It's not normal behavior by any means, nor is it the kind of thing that one would ever expect to repeat itself."

What is weird is that each generation of vandals were unaware of the previous desecration. And what is even more of a mystery is that these acts of defilement continued to be forgotten. If the Pierce Tomb is in fact cursed, the next scheduled skeletal sacrilege is scheduled for 2025.

As a paranormal researcher, I've seen history repeat itself and I wouldn't be surprised if these acts of vandalism are somehow tied to a postmortem curse of some sorts. In other words, are the ghosts of Old Hill Burying Ground responsible or is it purely coincidental?

Robert Ellis Cahill, known for his paranormal work in Salem, recounted how his investigator friend Brian captured a photo of what appeared to be Colonel Moses Titcomb's disembodied head poking out of the ground in front of his gravestone. The photo is reproduced in Cahill's book *Haunted Happenings* and is juxtaposed with a portrait of Titcomb. Cahill mused that Titicomb's ghost peeks out on moonlit nights to "see what is going on."

In the book, Cahill mentioned the ghosts associated with the Pierce Tomb at Old Hill Burying Ground. In fact, his investigator friend spotted two residual hauntings leaving the crypt using infrared binoculars. "I watched them leave a tomb and walk to the rock wall that faces the street overlooking Frog Pond," Cahill, who recently passed, reported in 1992. "There was nothing spectacular about them. I took photos, but they came out as blurs on the infrared film. They seemed to walk through the stone wall and then return to the tomb."

My friend Brian Gerraughty, a regular on my "Graveyard Getaways" tours, also encountered spirits near the Pierce Tomb. "Several years back around the time I first started to investigate, our group got some pretty solid responses on the spirit box from the ghost of a young boy who was reported to have drowned in a well," Gerraughty told me. "They were along the lines of 'it's dark, it's cold.' We got some pretty solid readings and responses to questions by the Pierce Tomb in response to some pretty specific questions regarding an incident that happened there after the occupants were interred in the crypt."

Gerraughty wouldn't go into detail but he implied that the spirits lingering around Pierce Tomb were extremely unhappy with the desecration. Gerraughty was unaware that the vandalism repeated itself but said that it "makes sense" to him because the tomb's ghostly inhabitants remembered what happened in the tomb in 1985.

Based on my experience in the Old Hill Burying Ground, I didn't experience anything paranormal. However, the scrapes caused by my "stop, drop and roll" incident did cut the visit short. As I was rolling down the hill with my camera in my hand, I did notice that the Pierce Tomb is now bricked in to avoid future vandalism.

While I didn't encounter any spirits lingering above ground, I was picking up major energy beneath me. At the time, I couldn't explain the vibration but it turns out there are reports of tunnels beneath Newburyport In hindsight, it makes total sense to me now.

"There's an intricate tunnel system under Burying Hill, through to High Street and down into town," wrote Cahill in *Haunted Happenings*. "Most Newburyporters know about it and some have entrances to it from their homes. And all of the locals concluded that it's haunted."

Apparently, Newburyport's underground tunnel system serves as a ghostly thoroughfare. "It's almost as if Newburyport was duplicated underground as a city and nobody seems to know for sure why, but they are widely reputed to be haunted." Cahill's friend Brian told him, adding that he heard ghostly reports from a family on High Street. "In the basement, a man discovered an entrance to the tunnels. That family constantly heard cries, weeping and wailing coming from the tunnels. He cemented up the entrance with bricks and mortar." The "terrible sounds" from below stopped after the man sealed up the underground tunnel's mysterious entrance.

While locals has incorrectly identified the underground labyrinth as "slave tunnels" it was probably used to smuggle goods from the wharf to avoid taxes. Pirates? Yep, Newburyport had them. However, they were given a less disparaging title. They were called "privateers."

The underground tunnel system could explain the ground's instability at Old Hill Burying Ground. There have been multiple reports of odd holes in the cemetery and, in at least one case involving a local paranormal group, there have been actual skeletal remains that have surfaced after a rainstorm.

During my visit to Old Hill Burying Ground, I didn't come face-to-face with the ghosts from Newburyport's dark past. However, I did sense an inexplicable energy lingering beneath the surface, almost as if the spirits were plotting a postmortem return. Will a new generation of vandals mysteriously return to the cemetery's Pierce Tomb to dance with the dead? If so, their next scheduled visit is 2025.

King's Chapel Burying Ground, located in Boston's "haunted corridor" next to the haunted Omni Parker House, is the city's oldest cemetery. *Photo by Frank C. Grace.*

Chapter 8
KING'S CHAPEL BURYING GROUND
Boston
Most Haunted: #8

"People are fascinated with cemeteries. It's like going to a historical house. King's Chapel offers the very, very old amongst a twenty-first-century city."
—Jim McCabe, Boston tour guide legend

Boston is a hotbed of paranormal activity. Whether you're a believer or not, there are more than a few skeletons in the city's collective closet. Many of those three-hundred-year-old secrets can be found in the buildings and landmarks scattered throughout the historic city. In fact, many of the spirits allegedly lingering in Boston might be a byproduct of the strong-willed New England desire to maintain the old buildings of the past, which act as lures to both visitors and ghosts. "Spirits are attracted to the places they lived in," opined the late Jim McCabe, who was a noted ghost lore expert in Boston. "I think what attracts ghosts up here is that you don't tear down the buildings."

Adam Berry, co-star of *Kindred Spirits* and a noted paranormal investigator formerly from *Ghost Hunters*, echoed McCabe's theory. "Because of the history, there are so many interesting places that could be investigated. It was one of the biggest seaports in the country and had tons of activity during the Revolutionary and Civil Wars. There must be spirits left behind, mulling about and checking out the status of the community they built way back when." During his four-year collegiate stint in Boston, the famed paranormal investigator said he fell in love with the Hub. "Boston's rich history and the singular fact that it was the cornerstone of the American Revolution makes it a city that is truly one of a kind," Berry said. "Why would anyone want to leave…even after they're dead?"

Some skeletons emerged when visitors least expected it. In January 2009, a tourist fell into an unmarked crypt at the Granary Burial Ground during a self-guided tour and got up close and personal with one of the cemetery's tombs, which measures eight by twelve feet in size and is believed to be the grave of an eighteenth-century selectman, Jonathan Armitage. The visitor wasn't hurt, nor did he fall into the actual crypt; instead, it was the stairway leading to the vault.

In 2007, a mysterious sinkhole emerged at King's Chapel Burial Ground, a 250-year-old cemetery dating back to 1757 near Government Center and across from the haunted Omni Parker House. "Beneath the crumbling earth are stairs leading down to the family crypt," reported the *Boston Herald* in January 2007. "It's unclear why this grave in particular is giving way, though time and weather are chief among the suspected causes." The sinkhole, which was blocked off from pedestrians with a black steel cage, continued to baffle the burial ground's conservators for years.

King's Chapel Burying Ground was the scene of several historical tales from the crypt, including reports of a man who was rumored to be buried alive in 1820.

One elderly woman strongly believed that a nineteenth-century property owner was buried six feet under by his family in an attempt to get possession of his wealth. An angry mob gathered around the burial ground, demanding that authorities exhume the body. Doctors investigated, and it was announced that he was dead as a doornail. However, the woman continued to believe that the death occurred as the result of him being buried alive.

In 1775, the lauded editor of the *Columbian Centinel*, Benjamin Russell, had an encounter with the supernatural when the historic cemetery on the corner of Tremont and School Streets was known as Stone Chapel. "It was part of my duty as an assistant in the domestic affairs of the family to have the care of the cow. One evening, after it was quite dark, I was driving the cow to her pasturage—the Common. Passing by the burial-ground, adjoining the Stone Chapel, I saw several lights that appeared to be springing from the earth, among the graves, and immediately sinking again to the ground. To my young imagination, they could be nothing but ghosts," Russell recounted in *The Pilgrims of Boston* by Thomas Bridgman.

Russell continued: "I left the cow to find her way to the Common, and ran home at my utmost speed. Having told my father the cause of my fright, he took me to the spot where the supposed ghosts were still leaping and playing their pranks. When, lo! there was the sexton, throwing out as he was digging fragments of decayed coffins. The phosphorus in the decayed wood blending with the peculiar state of the atmosphere, presented the appearance that had completely unstrung my nerves, and terrified me beyond description. I was never afterwards troubled with the fear of ghosts."

While most ghost lore experts name Boston Common's Central Burying Ground as the most haunted cemetery in the Hub, the older King's Chapel Burying Ground—built in 1630 and hosting a slew of Puritan founders, including Governor John Winthrop, Reverend John Cotton and Mary Chilton (the first woman to walk off the Mayflower)—boasts a few ghostly legends of its own. Included in these is the strange story of roaming spirits looking for their markers. In 1810, there was a switcheroo of sorts when the superintendent of burials moved most of the headstones at the cemetery and laid them out in neat rows closer to the center of the yard. The legend states that the moving of the headstones confused the spirits so much that ever since they've wandered aimlessly looking for their graves.

Incidentally, the cemetery is built adjacent to King's Chapel, an Anglican church. Many of the big-name burials were Puritan elders who left England in search of religious freedom. Ironically, their final resting place is next to the church they fled.

In addition to the wandering-ghost myth, a macabre story associated with the churchyard states that a woman is buried there whose head was cut off and placed between her legs. The story goes that the carpenter built the woman's coffin too small and, in an attempt to cover his blunder, decapitated the corpse, placed the head inside the coffin and nailed the lid shut. No proof exists as to the legend's truth.

Another story associated with the churchyard centers on an unmarked grave at the rear of the cemetery. Although the gravestone has no name, many believe it's the final resting place of the infamous pirate Captain Kidd. While the salty dog was definitely arrested in Boston in 1701 and was hanged and buried in the city, little proof exists to either support or disprove the idea that he was interred next to King's Chapel. Of course, it doesn't stop the pirate-themed ghost stories. "There are some grave-goers who swear that Kidd's spirit can be summoned late at night, during the bewitching hour, and seen patrolling Boston's ancient burying ground," wrote Christopher Forest in *Boston's Haunted History*. "Legend has it that Kidd is the most restless of the historic burial ground's denizens," added Joseph Mont and Marcia Weaver in the *Ghosts of Boston*. "Should the gate be left open at its Tremont Street entrance, visitors are ill advised to trespass after dark."

In addition to the mischievous pirate spirit, many visitors claimed to have problems with their cameras and recording devices when visiting the site. Some have noticed that their video footage was mysteriously deleted and batteries drained while walking in the cemetery. After leaving the so-called energy vortex, their electronic devices returned to normal.

Why does so much ghost lore surround the old-school burial ground? "People are fascinated with cemeteries," explained Jim McCabe in a 2007 interview with the *Boston Herald*. "It's like going to a historical house. King's Chapel offers the very, very old amongst a twenty-first-century city. The rest of the country just doesn't have the sense of history we do."

Spirits at King's Chapel? It's possible. "There are some who opine that every Boston landmark is haunted," wrote Holly Nadler in *Ghosts of Boston Town*. While Russell had a scientific explanation disproving his childhood ghost story, others believe that Boston has been the epicenter of supernatural activity since the Puritans set foot on the hallowed ground in the early 1600s.

Witch-trials victim George Jacobs is said to haunt the Rebecca Nurse Homestead Cemetery in Danvers. *Photo by Sam Baltrusis.*

Chapter 9
REBECCA NURSE HOMESTEAD CEMETERY
Danvers
Most Haunted: #9

"There have been reports of an apparent phantom in the burial ground."
—*Lee Holloway,* Ghosts of the Salem Witch Trials

If it's true that there is a postmortem unrest associated with the proper burial of skeletal remains, then witch-trials victim George Jacobs may be hanging around the Rebecca Nurse Homestead cemetery in Danvers. The backstory behind what historians believe could be the seventy-two-year-old farmer's remains is a strange one.

"From what I hear, the bones were dug up and kept in a box for a long time at the Danvers Historical Society," explained Kelly Daniell, archivist with the Peabody Historical Society. "They were interred where we think Rebecca Nurse was buried."

Based on representations of Jacobs, specifically in Arthur Miller's *The Crucible*, the elderly man was thrown under the ox cart by the Salem Village community as well as his family. Not only was Jacobs accused of being a wizard but his son George Jacobs Jr. and his daughter-in-law Rebecca were brought in for questioning along with his granddaughter Margaret.

In the pre-trial hearings of Jacobs Sr. at Beadle's Tavern, Margaret confessed under pressure from authorities to finger her grandfather and the Rev. George Burroughs, a former minister of Salem Village who was also hanged. Although she later recanted the coerced confession, Jacobs was executed on August 19, 1692.

Meanwhile, the twelve-year-old Margaret barely escaped execution because she was too ill to stand trial. With his case, the hysteria literally pitted family members against each other. However, it was the granddaughter—not the strong-willed Jacobs—who seemed devastated by the pre-trial hearings.

The famous painting by Thompkins H. Matteson from 1855 entitled the *Trial of George Jacobs, August 5, 1692,* captured the emotion of the interrogation. However, it's somewhat inaccurate. Jacobs is portrayed as a vulnerable elderly man who was apparently brought to his knees when he was accused of witchcraft.

His gravestone, memorializing what is believed to be his remains at the Rebecca Nurse Homestead cemetery in Danvers, captures the essence of Jacobs's defiant character. "Well burn me, or hang me," Jacobs emoted at his examination. "I will stand in the truth of Christ."

He was executed in 1692 and his famous words are etched into his memorial marker. However, his execution wasn't the last time Jacobs was spotted.

According to Charles W. Upham, Jacobs's bones were exhumed in the 1800s and then buried back in the same spot in present-day Danversport next to the river. "The tradition has descended through the family, that the body, after having been obtained at the place of execution, was strapped by a young grandson on the back of a horse, brought home to the farm, and buried beneath the shade of his own trees," explained Upham in *Salem Witchcraft*. "Two sunken and weather-worn stones marked the spot. There the remains rested until 1864, when they were exhumed."

The body, said to have a tall skeletal frame, was accidentally uncovered again in the early 1950s by bulldozers after Jacobs's property had been sold. The remains were kept in a winter crypt at a local cemetery and then handed over to historian Richard Trask in the late 1960s. "Safeguarded for years by Danvers officials, the skeleton was quietly reburied on the Rebecca Nurse farm, complete with replica seventeenth-century coffin and gravestone, in 1992," confirmed Emerson W. Baker in *A Storm of Witchcraft*. "Although analysis of the remains established that they were those of an old man and generally fit Jacob's description, it will never know whether they really were those of Jacobs."

For the record, Trask "safeguarded" the bones in a glass case designed for an antique ship and stored them in his bedroom until giving them a proper burial in 1992. Yes, it's an out-of-the-box approach to storing ancient remains.

Locals claimed that the ghost of George Jacobs once haunted the location of his former home and gravesite on Margin Street in Danvers. "Following the 1950s disinterment, there were no further sightings of Jacobs's spirit near the river, but many believe the convicted wizard's spirit follows his bones," wrote Lee Holloway in the online article, *Ghosts of the Salem Witch Trials*. "The isolated family graveyard in which George Jacobs now lies is situated in a copse of trees on the Rebecca Nurse homestead and for several years, there have been reports of an apparent phantom in the burial ground."

Holloway reported that there have been multiple sightings of a male spirit lurking in the wooded area behind the cemetery. "One such sighting occurred August 19, 1999, when a group of visitors walking from the house toward the cemetery saw what one later described as 'a man in dark clothes.' They initially assumed it was one of the Danvers Alarm List militiamen who operate the Nurse farm, but as they neared the burial ground, the figure vanished," she wrote, adding that one of the women who spotted the spirit checked with a worker in the gift shop. "I'm the only one on the estate today," the volunteer maintained. "Maybe it was the ghost of old George Jacobs."

Strangely, the face-to-face encounter was on the anniversary of Jacobs's execution. He was hanged at Proctor's Ledge on August 19, 1692.

Based on a recent visit to the cemetery behind the Nurse property, I strongly believe that the land is haunted, specifically near the memorial which also includes the remains of several Putnam family members. Walking into the Nurse family burial ground, you could feel an energy shift. I also sensed a male presence there and actually saw an outline of a man when I shot photos of Jacobs's gravestone.

It felt like someone was peering at me from the woods behind the burial ground. Was it Jacobs? Perhaps. Based on ghost lore, hauntings have been associated with the lack of proper burial or a later desecration of the grave. Yes, it's possible that the witch-trials victim is watching over his remains and lurking in the shadows of the wooded area behind them.

The Parson Barnard House in North Andover was featured on Destination America's *Haunted Towns. Photo by Frank C. Grace.*

Chapter 10
OLD BURIAL GROUND
North Andover
Most Haunted: #10

"Pennies were flying through the air."

—Gregg Pascoe, Parson Barnard's House caretaker

Did Thomas Barnard, the assistant minister to the Rev. Francis Dane in Andover during the witch trials of 1692, get a bum rap? Gregg Pascoe, the caretaker of the Parson Barnard House in present-day North Andover, believes he did.

"For many years people unfairly judged him because they assumed he was a driving factor during the Salem witch trials, particularly in the episode that happened here where over fifty people were accused," Pascoe told me during a tour of the historic property. "But that's not the case."

Dane, on the other hand, was involved in a witch trial thirty years prior where he testified against spectral evidence.

While the seventy-six-year-old Dane was vehemently opposed to the trials that were unfolding in nearby Salem Village, the young Barnard was fresh out of Harvard and wanted to make a name for himself at the parsonage. Historians believed that the Rev. Barnard invited two of the afflicted girls—Mary Walcott and Ann Putnam Jr.—to attend the prayer meetings that included "touch tests" involving Andover's upper crust.

Pascoe said Barnard delivered the opening prayer at the infamous church service in September 1692 when all hell broke loose. "The afflicted girls started touching people and they ended up arresting seventeen people for witchcraft on the spot," Pascoe said. "Because he started the service, people assumed that Barnard sanctioned the whole process and was in on bringing in the girls. He wasn't."

With the "touch test," the afflicted would put their hands on the innocent people of Andover and if they stopped having a fit then that townsperson was a witch. Oddly, several members of the Reverend Dane's family were accused using this so-called test including his two daughters and five of his grandchildren.

People assumed that Barnard was feuding with Dane and then orchestrated the "touch test" surprise. "In reality, Barnard wasn't an instigator during the church service," Pascoe explained. "He was just as surprised as everybody else."

Pascoe said the afflicted girls were like rock stars and the locals, including the extremely ill Timothy Swan, started a whole second wave of accusations. Because Barnard went to Harvard, people automatically assumed that he and the Rev. Cotton Mather were somehow in cahoots. "I'm sure they knew each other but I don't think they were buddies at Harvard," Pascoe said.

Were Barnard and Dane feuding reverends? It's possible. When Andover hired Barnard in 1682, they stopped paying Dane and gave the new minister in town a full salary. After Dane protested to officials in Boston, the church was required to split Barnard's pay with Dane. Of course, the town complied with the order.

However, they divided the money unevenly. "They both were unhappy," Pascoe told me. "Barnard felt like he should get a full salary and so did Dane."

When Pascoe gave tours at the Parson Barnard House, he initially portrayed the reverend as a bad guy. "I started to incorporate the information that he was somehow a conspirator," the caretaker told me. "Every time I did that, the fire alarms in the house would mysteriously go off."

Pascoe took the alarms as a sign from beyond. "At that point, I started to question the information about Barnard. I felt like it wasn't correct. I started to incorporate the correct history on my tours and the fire alarms stopped going off. I believe it's him trying to correct me."

The elderly Dane was the driving force behind putting a stop to the trials in Andover. In fact, he wrote a petition in October 1692 addressing what he believed to be forced confessions of guilt made by the victims during the "touch test" frenzy. Fifty people were accused of witchcraft in Andover during the witch trials and it's estimated that eighty percent of the town's residents had been affected in some way by the hysteria.

Tim Weisberg, a paranormal investigator and co-host of Spooky Southcoast, echoed Pascoe's theory. "Although some of the original research indicated that Barnard was a student of Cotton Mather and one of the real instigators behind the witch trials, the society at the Parson Barnard House has been doing more research over the years and uncovered that Barnard actually fought to end the trials, and came to the defense of many of the accused," he confirmed.

Weisberg, who also investigated the Old Burial Ground across the street from the Parson Barnard House, believes that Barnard has been upset with how he has been portrayed and wants people know the truth. "We got a lot of interaction during our last investigation when it came to discussing that notion with what we believe was his spirit," Weisberg continued, adding that the most profound spirit communication occurred in the nearby cemetery which is where both the reverend and witch-trials accuser, Timothy Swan, are buried.

Built in 1715, the Parson Barnard House in North Andover was a later-in-life homestead for the reverend who was wrongly blamed as an instigator during the Salem witch trials. Barnard's previous home, the town's parsonage in Andover, mysteriously caught on fire and burned to the ground. "He lived here for three years," Pascoe told me as we explored the three-hundred-year-old property. "They started work on it in 1714 and it was completed one year later."

Pascoe isn't exactly sure how the reverend passed. "I heard that he had an illness but I've also read that he had a stroke," the caretaker told me. Pascoe doesn't know the details of Barnard's death. But, he's convinced the home's first owner is lingering there in the afterlife.

When Pascoe first moved into the house in 2012, he heard a disembodied voice utter his name in the attic. "I had just moved in and I was giving family members a tour of the house," he recalled. "When I walked up the stairs, I heard my name."

The caretaker said the paranormal activity continued for years. Walking through the structure was like stepping back in time. Each step had a story.

During my tour with Pascoe, I noticed that there was dried sage hanging throughout the structure which added to its already-eerie aesthetic. "Back in their day, sage was an herb that they used for flavoring food and medicinal purposes. They even dyed clothing with some herbs," Pascoe said. "It wasn't unusual for dried sage to be hanging around the house."

When I asked Pascoe if colonists used sage to ward off spirits back in the 1700s, he shrugged. "I don't think it was used to cleanse homes in that era," he said. "At the same time, everybody believed in witchcraft back then. Did they know it could be used for cleansing? Probably. It could have been a folksy wisdom that they knew about."

In addition to Pascoe's first-hand experiences in the attic and the fire alarm sounding off when he incorrectly told Barnard's story, the caretaker said the ghostly activity intensified when he invited paranormal investigators and mediums to check out the property.

He watched in awe when he saw a penny being slung by a disembodied spirit in the Parson Barnard House. "There were tons of coins in this house," he told me. "I figured the former caretaker left them." Pascoe joked that he collected the loose change for beer money but he missed a few.

Pascoe said he was shocked when the resident ghosts figured out how to manipulate the coins. "Pennies were flying through the air," he told me.

The property also showcases an original seventeenth-century book called *Concordance* owned by the reverend. "One medium asked me is she could touch it," Pascoe said. "She then heard a male voice say 'don't touch my book' and she quickly pulled away."

In 2017, I recommended the Parson Barnard House to the producers of the television show, *Haunted Towns*. One of the investigators from the Tennessee Wraith Chasers, Steven "Doogie" McDougal, was terrorized in the structure's attic. While sitting in a chair, his leg was tugged. Oddly, the word "yank" appeared on the Ovilus when he was sitting in isolation.

Weisberg, one of the producers from the TV show, set up an investigation after watching Doogie appear to be physically accosted by an unseen force. "I found out about the Parson Barnard House through working on *Haunted Towns*," Weisberg told Wicked Local. "When I saw how the Salem episode turned out, and the experiences the cast had at the Parson Barnard House, I knew I wanted to check it out."

Pascoe said Weisberg's investigation was intense. "He asked the ghost to move this penny," he said, showing me the coin that mysteriously was thrown at an investigator. Weisberg set up his flashlight on the dresser as he asked the entity to move the penny. The caretaker said the flashlight moved instead.

"The penny didn't move but the spirit energy moved the flashlight," Pascoe added.

#11

Hammond Castle is located at 80 Hesperus Ave. in Gloucester. *Photo by Ryan Miner.*

Chapter 11
HAMMOND CASTLE
Gloucester
Most Haunted: #11

"The big story about this place when I was a kid is that Hammond himself haunted the grounds."
—*Josh Gates, "Ghost Hunters" guest investigator*

When my friend and former research assistant Andrew Warburton and I visited Hammond Castle in Gloucester back in July 2012, I heard a disembodied voice say "look" in the library, which historians call the "whisper" room. It led me to a picture of Henry Davis Sleeper.

Was it Sleeper's ghost? Probably not. However, I wouldn't be surprised if it was the structure's former owner was trying to reach out to me to let me know that his friend Sleeper had designed the room.

Inventor John Hays Hammond, Jr. built this breathtaking medieval-style castle in the late 1920s. Marrying his wife Irene Fenton late in his life, the eccentric gentleman used the mansion as a laboratory and private residence until his death in 1956. In fact, he's buried in a crypt tucked away on the property and is rumored to be among the several wayward spirits who haunt the house. Hammond had an odd desire to be reincarnated as a cat and many believe the black feline who roamed the grounds and set up shop in his favorite chair in the library was, in fact, Hammond himself.

The mad scientist collected bizarre antiques, like the skull of a seaman from Christopher Columbus' crew, and it's said that some of the artifacts are enchanted. He was also fascinated by spiritualism and there's an area known as the "dead spot," marked by a chair, where Hammond hosted psychic mediums. Items in the castle inexplicably disappear and reappear. A full-bodied apparition has been seen in the organ loft and a red-haired female specter has popped up among guests at weddings held at the castle.

Henry Davis Sleeper, the legendary designer who built Eastern Point's Beauport, was a regular at Hammond Castle. In fact, Sleeper designed the inventor's favorite spot, known as the "whisper room," where people have heard disembodied voices from beyond.

I first visited the haunted castle a few weeks before Syfy's *Ghost Hunters* was scheduled to investigate. Oddly, two days after my initial trip to Gloucester, I was scheduled to interview one of the show's hosts, Adam Berry, in Provincetown. He was preparing for a top-secret shoot.

"Are you investigating Hammond Castle?" I asked Berry. He nodded but couldn't give any details. He was shocked that I intuitively knew that *Ghost Hunters* was heading to Gloucester.

For the record, I did get a heads up from John Pettibone, the curator and director of the haunted hot spot. But I was also mysteriously called to the location.

Pettibone was a bit freaked out when I told him that I write historical-based ghost books and asked if the castle was paranormally active. "Is the castle haunted? We'll find out in a few weeks," Pettibone told me in 2012. "The team from TAPS is doing the investigation. I feel strongly that Hammond would have approved of their scientific approach to paranormal investigations."

Pettibone told me that Hammond and his wife were ghost hunters before the fad became a pop culture phenomenon. In many ways, the couple were trailblazers paving the way for respected, contemporary investigators like The Atlantic Paranormal Society.

"Hammond firmly believed that when you bring back architectural items that you're bringing back the spirit of the original owner," Pettibone explained to the TAPS team on Syfy's *Ghost Hunters*. "John Hammond did paranormal experiments using his Faraday Cage. His wife was an astrologer and a psychic. They did séances here. We had John Hammond seen by a school group on the balcony in the Great Hall. We had his wife seen at a window."

The episode, which aired in November 2012, was a throwback to the old-school *Ghost Hunters* investigations that presented some convincing evidence. Josh Gates, host of Syfy's *Destination Truth* and the Travel Channel's *Expedition Unknown*, joined the team and confirmed that he grew up close to Gloucester in nearby Manchester-by-the-Sea. "There's always been ghost stories here since I was a kid. I almost had my prom here," Gates joked. "It was deemed too scary to have a prom at so we didn't."

According to Pettibone, guests in the library or "whisper room" report hearing voices speaking foreign languages. Books from Hammond's collection of the occult have flown off shelves without explanation. Visitors have also taken mysterious photos in the Great Hall of what looked like orbs with distinct heads.

Employees told the *Ghost Hunters* team that Hammond's medieval bedroom on the second floor is also extremely active. "Some people who walk in there feel really uneasy," said Hammond Castle employee Linda Rose. "They feel cool. Their hair would stand up on end. There was another gentleman that went in there and felt something go through him."

Jay Craveiro, also a staffer at the Hammond Castle, said a girl with a tour group had a face-to-face encounter with a spirit on the second floor near the medieval bedroom. According to Craveiro, her blood-curdling scream echoed throughout the castle. "She said she saw a hand reach toward her face while the staff was downstairs," Craveiro explained. "She just started running all the way through the castle and right out of the front door. She refused to come back into the building."

In addition to the eyewitness accounts, there's a series of photos of what appears to be a full-bodied apparition walking up the castle's staircase. "It has a little bit of a definition and when you put the photos together it appears to move up the steps almost as if you can see an end of a pant leg moving its foot up each step," remarked Kris Gurksnis, a Salem-based visitor to Hammond Castle.

The TAPS team's actual investigation of the historic structure is arguably one of the *Ghost Hunters* crew's more entertaining shows. In its show recap, Syfy reported the following: "During the investigation, Dave and Tango hear a voice, while Amy and Adam hear a voice and whistling in the room with them. Meanwhile, K.J. and Britt have great communication with a spirit using a rim pod. Not only do Jason and Steve hear strange voices behind them, but also feet walking behind them."

To reiterate the myth that Hammond would reincarnate as a feline, a cat appeared out of nowhere during the investigation. "Josh and Ashley get some great responses to their questions on the K2 meter, and actually give chase to a voice. When they move to the library, the chandelier begins swinging aggressively without any cause," Syfy described. "As Josh says, it's like a cliché haunted house."

Inventor John Hays Hammond, Jr. was buried on the grounds of his medieval-style castle. The eccentric had an odd desire to be reincarnated as a cat and many believe he succeeded. *Photo by Frank C. Grace.*

When asked how the investigation was unfolding, Gates said "it was awesome. We heard voices and one of them came two feet behind us. I was able to register what it was and where it was coming from and still hear and analyze it," the TV host said. "All of the different teams are having similar experiences. It's a good, all-round case for everybody."

Gates was right. The K2 meter lit up on command during a call-and-response session near the so-called "dead spot" in the Great Hall. There was also a recording of residual chatter of what clearly sounded like a cocktail party from another era. The moving chandelier was a bit shocking during Ashley Troub and Gates's trek through the Great Hall.

"The big story about this place when I was a kid is that Hammond himself haunted the grounds," Gates said during the investigation.

When Jason Hawes and Steve Gonsalves turned on their digital recorder, they picked up a Class A electronic-voice phenomenon. It was a male voice and it clearly said: "Hammond." Pettibone was visibly excited when he heard the EVP during the reveal. "I don't hear it as a question," the curator responded. "I hear it as a statement."

Pettibone said he was convinced by the TAPS crew's findings. "Is John Hammond still here? Is Irene still here? I am just amazed what came out," Pettibone gushed. "Someone is trying to let us know they're still here."

Boston's second-oldest cemetery, Copp's Hill boasts the remains of two important figures from the Salem witch trials including Cotton and Increase Mather. *Photo by Sam Baltrusis.*

Chapter 12
COPP'S HILL CEMETERY
Boston
Most Haunted: #12

"There definitely were tunnels underneath the North End."
—Peter Muise, New England Folklore blog

Based purely on aesthetic, Boston's North End should be haunted. In fact, horror writer H.P. Lovecraft believed the neighborhood was fertile ground for the supernatural. In *Pickman's Model*, the author convincingly wrote about the inexplicable magic of the North End's spirited underbelly, adding that "the whole North End once had a set of tunnels that kept certain people in touch with each other's houses, and the burying ground and the sea." He also talked about the lack of ghosts in Boston's Back Bay saying the newly created land around Newbury Street hasn't been around long enough "to pick up memories and attract local spirits."

The Rev. Cotton Mather, along with his influential family members including his Harvard president father Increase, is buried in the Mather Tomb in the Copp's Hill Cemetery in the North End. "The second-oldest cemetery in Boston, Copp's Hill was established in 1659 and is filled with famous figures such as Cotton and Increase Mather, as well as former slaves and revolutionary soldiers," reported the website *OnlyInYourState*. "Some say the hallowed ground is haunted by the spirit of Increase Mather, a fierce and imposing colonial preacher who condemned many of the so-called Salem witches to hell."

While the blogger probably mixed up the Harvard president with his witch-hunting son, the legend associated with the lingering spirit at Copp's Hill suggests it's the Rev. Cotton Mather and not his dad, Increase. "Some visitors see glowing orbs of light appear amongst the tombstones, while others say they have felt unseen bodies brush against them in the dark," the website claimed.

Is Copp's Hill Cemetery haunted by Cotton? It's possible. However, locals in the North End notoriously remain tight-lipped about the neighborhood's ghost lore.

Michael Baker, head of the group called the New England Center for the Advancement of Paranormal Science (NECAPS) and member of Para-Boston, leaves no gravestone unturned when he investigates a so-called haunted location, which includes a few of the old structures in the North End. Baker said he's heard very few reports of ghosts in the historic buildings surrounding Copp's Hill Cemetery. Why? He believes it's a cultural thing.

"The North End seems a bit devoid of claims," Baker said when asked about the lack of alleged paranormal activity in the historically Italian neighborhood. "I have always felt much of it has to do with the religious views of the people who live there. There are a lot of old-school Italian families there, people who tend to be well embedded in religious culture. I have noticed that this old-world approach to religion often brings with it an unspoken rule about dabbling in or acknowledging things related to the paranormal."

Oddly, one of Boston's more infamous made-up ghost stories involves a man leaving his home from Middle Street in the North End. William Austin's Peter Rugg literary character—who stubbornly rode his horse into a thunderstorm in 1770 and was cursed to drive his carriage until the end of time—was completely fabricated. However, people over the years have reportedly spotted the ghostly man with his daughter by his side frantically trying to make the trek back to Boston.

According to the legend, Rugg was visiting Concord with his daughter and stopped by a tavern recommended to him by a longtime friend before heading back to Boston. A violent thunderstorm was heading in their direction and the watering hole's owner insisted that Rugg and his daughter stay the night. Rugg, a notoriously defiant old man, refused the offer and headed directly into the storm. The horse and its driver never returned to Boston. However, people claimed to have seen what was called "the Stormbreeder," a phantom carriage driven by Rugg and considered to be the precursor to a thunderstorm, all over New England. One man in Connecticut said he had a face-to-face encounter with the ghost. "I have lost the road to Boston. My name is Peter Rugg," the specter supposedly said before vanishing into thin air.

For many, the only real ghosts that exist are the ones that haunt the insides of their heads.

"There are some claims in the North End," continued Baker. "I know there are stories about the tunnels there. I have had a few calls from the North End over the years, but unfortunately they never amounted to anything significant."

Baker isn't ruling out the possibility of ghosts in the North End. However, he hasn't found anything substantial while investigating there and finds the locals to be unusually tight-lipped. "I know several old Italian families and they won't even embrace a discussion about ghosts," he said. "To them it's religiously forbidden. Of course, this is just my speculation but it's a pattern I've seen in people I speak with."

While the North End is mysteriously devoid of reported ghost sightings, the legends associated with its series of rumored underground tunnels seem to be based on reported fact. "There definitely were tunnels underneath the North End," explained Peter Muise, author of *Legends and Lore of the North Shore*. "For example, in the nineteenth century construction workers discovered that a house at 453 Commercial St. had an archway in its cellar that connected to a large tunnel. It led from Commercial Street up toward Salem Street. Unfortunately this house was demolished in 1906 and the tunnel entrance along with it."

Who built the tunnels? Muise said they were probably built in the 1700s by Thomas Gruchy, a privateer who became wealthy from raiding Spanish ships. "He invested his loot in several Boston businesses, including a distillery, a warehouse and several wharves. His wealth was excessive even for a privateer, and many of his neighbors suspected that he was somehow smuggling goods into Boston without having to pay the British tariffs. Despite his shady background he became a prominent member of Boston society. He purchased the Salem Street mansion of former Governor Phipps in 1745, threw lavish parties, and became a congregant at the Old North Church. Four plaster angels that he looted from a French ship still decorate the church today."

Gruchy mysteriously disappeared in the 1700s and left behind a legacy of underground tunnels and stolen goods. "At the height of his wealth and popularity Gruchy vanished from Boston and was never seen again," Muise explained. "It's believed that he was smuggling goods past the British using a series of underground tunnels, and fled town when they discovered what he was doing. Sadly his mansion on Salem Street was torn down years ago."

Muise said that many secrets are buried beneath the North End's blood-stained soil. "A few other North End tunnels have been found," he said. "A book from 1817 mentions a tunnel under a house on Lynn Street, and a guide to Boston architecture notes that the cellar of a house on Salem Street still has an entrance to a tunnel in its basement. It has been bricked off so it's not clear where the tunnel goes or what it was used for."

Perhaps the ghosts of the North End are hiding in these hidden tunnels? Yes, it's possible that they're lurking in the shadows beneath the cobblestone streets traveled by thousands of tourists flocking to a neighborhood famous for its old-school Italian eateries, Paul Revere and the Mather family's tomb.

Entrance to Riverside Cemetery in Barre. *Photo by Jason Baker*.

Chapter 13
RIVERSIDE CEMETERY
Barre
Most Haunted: #13

"Heaven won't take me."
    —EVP captured by Joni Mayhan, author and paranormal investigator

As we stepped into the cemetery, it was apparent that something bad once happened there. The energy hung in the air like a bank of fog, surging around us as if trying to get our attention. I allowed the energy to connect and immediately saw a young woman who feared for her life. I knew in an instant that she lost her life in this forest.

The land has a way of holding onto energy. Some of it is good. When you go there, you feel instantly comfortable. Other places hold onto other emotions. As a paranormal investigator, I recognize much of it as residual energy. It isn't necessarily haunted in the sense that most people identify with. It's just there, resounding like an imprint on the land.

For someone with metaphysical gifts, it's apparent. We feel the energy and find ourselves identifying it before we even notice the scenery. One such place is the former town of Coldbrook Village.

Coldbrook Springs was once a bustling town with two hotels, a bowling alley, a blacksmith shop, post office, billiard hall, a box mill, school, and nearly 35 houses. It was removed in the 1930s as part of the Quabbin Reservoir project. The state bought all of the buildings and demolished them to provide a clean watershed for the Ware River, which flows into the Quabbin Reservoir and provides drinking water to Boston and its suburbs. People were relocated to nearby towns of Oakham, Barre and Hubbardston, and the town simply ceased to exist.

Besides a few foundations, the cemetery is virtually all that remains of the old town. We walked the grounds, taking in the mixture of old and new headstones. Birds chirped in the distance as the wind rustled through the tops of the tall pines. At the back of the cemetery we found a monument to the Naramore children, who were killed by their own mother in 1901. We spend a quiet moment reading the inscription.

Poverty stricken and living with an abusive husband, Elizabeth Naramore went to the town for help. When officials visited the residence, they determined that the children would need to be put into foster homes. Before they could do that, Elizabeth killed them, from oldest to youngest, and then attempted unsuccessfully to commit suicide. A monument was erected in the 1990s to remember the lost children. It's hard to stand there and not feel a rush of emotion. Over time, the stone has gained a collection of toys and small cars, left by saddened visitors.

As we walked back towards the entrance, I was drawn to a group of three tombstones.

They were old and faded, the words difficult to make out on the worn slate stone. The first stone listed the name of a Catherine Sibley, who lived from 1805 to 1874. Beside her grave was the grave of her husband, Captain Charles Sibley, who lived from 1808 to 1849. And sadly, beside his was the grave of their four children. This was what caused me to pause.

They were listed, one after another, telling a heartbreaking story.

- James died on October 9, 1843 at nine months old.
- Catherine died on September 19, 1847 at six years, five months.
- Mary died the day after her sister, on September 20, 1847 at the age of two years, seven months.
- Charles died the day after Christmas on the same year, December 26, 1847 at the age of twelve years, seven months.

We just stood there, taking it all in, trying to wrap our minds around the tragedy of losing four children, two of whom died within a day of one another. How did they die? Was there a horrible disease that swept through the area, taking their children one by one, teasing them to believe that one would survive, only to have him taken from them the day after Christmas? My heart went out to their parents.

The Naramore grave in Riverside Cemetery in Barre is usually surrounded by toys and offerings to the victims of the filicide. *Photo by Jason Baker.*

I'm always very respectful of the dead, and with this comes a sense of compassion. As a paranormal investigator, I know that not all of the souls pass on like they're supposed to. When faced with a tragic death, some lose their way and become earthbound. We wanted to make sure this wasn't the case. We pulled out our digital recorders and conducted a short EVP session.

"Captain Sibley, are you still here?" Sandy asked.

The response was heart wrenching. "Yes. Heaven won't take me."

The EVP is faint and must be listened to with headphones on high volume. For reasons I can't explain, the audio has faded over the years, perhaps from being transferred too many times, or possibly for other reasons. Maybe I was the only one meant to hear it.

After listening to it, I couldn't stop thinking about this poor family and the possibility that the father was still lingering around his grave over one-hundred and sixty years later. I went back to his grave the following week.

In the quiet of the cemetery, I sat beside his headstone and just talked to him. I didn't know if he was listening or not, but I wanted to help him if I could. I told him about the natural process of what happens to us after death.

"When we die, we're supposed to cross over into the white light, moving to the place where we're supposed to go. Some people call it Heaven," I said. I looked around at the quiet bank of trees, wondering if he was there, or if I was simply talking to myself. I had to continue though.

My voice sounded like a prayer as I began speaking again. "Look for the white light. It's right above you. All your family is waiting for you. Call out to them to help you cross through." I took a deep breath and then added something I hoped would help. "God loves you and welcomes you with open arms. Go find the peace and serenity you deserve." And then I cried.

I went back several weeks later to see if he was still there. I turned on my digital voice recorder and asked again. "Captain Sibley, are you still here?" Later when I listened to the recording, all I heard was the sound of birds chirping in the background. If he was still there, he wasn't responding. I hoped he'd listened to my advice and found the peace he so deserved. For insurance, a year later I brought a psychic medium to the cemetery and he crossed over five souls. My hope was that if Captain Sibley hadn't crossed over initially, that he'd gone when the psychic medium gave him another opportunity. Either way, I truly feel he finally found his way.

The story would have ended there if I'd been able to let it go. Thoughts of the Sibley family haunted me. I couldn't get them off my mind. I reached out to a friend who has a knack for researching and she was able to provide me with more information. She filled in many of the details for me, fleshing out the bare-boned tragedy and giving it life.

The Sibleys had a long history in Massachusetts. They arrived in Salem in 1629, quickly becoming a very prominent family. They boasted statesmen and soldiers of the Revolutionary War, as well as being prosperous business owners. An early relative of Charles Sibley's was Mary Woodrow Sibley, who allegedly showed

Tituba and Indian John how to make the urine cakes used to test for witches during the Salem Witch Trials.

Nearly two centuries later, Charles Sibley was born in 1808, the youngest of five siblings. The family relocated to Barre, Massachusetts while he was a child, setting up a homestead just outside of Coldbrook Springs. When he was 25 years-old, he married a woman named Catharine Brigham who was three years his senior. He was listed as "Captain Sibley" on his gravestone, but no information could be found about any military services. In colonial times, this was often added to the name because of the family's past military service.

The unspeakable story of the Naramore family and the events of March 21, 1901 has been laid to rest with the bodies of the six children who were buried in the paupers' corner of Riverside Cemetery on Granger Road. *Photo by Jason Baker.*

They were married for two years before having their first child, a son they named Charles, after his father. Three years later, they would have another son named Nelson. Daughter, Catherine, was born two afterward, named after her mother. The following year, they would add another son, James, to the family, but he would die of whooping cough before his first birthday. In 1845, they would have a second daughter they named Mary. And in 1848 they would have their last child, who they would also name Charles.

They would lose all but two of their children soon after to dysentery.

Dying of dysentery was a very horrible way to go. An inflammation of the lower intestines would lead to a high fever and painful, never-ending diarrhea. Left untreated, the victim would become dehydrated and eventually succumb to the infection. It is often caused by consuming contaminated food or water, or from poor hygiene. Charles himself would die two years later from Typhoid Fever, after being sick for eight straight days.

Charles' wife, Catherine would live to be sixty-nine, dying in 1874 in Boston. Her death certificate listed paralysis as the cause of death, although I'm sure there's more to the story. Sons, Nelson and Charles (the second) would survive both of their parents. Nelson married in 1870 and died in 1900. Charles married in 1882 and died sometime after 1930 in Highgate, Vermont. His occupation was listed as a paper carrier.

There is still so much I don't know about the Sibley family, and I'm certain this won't be the last time I'll think of them. One thing is certain, I feel as though I was led to his grave for a reason. Maybe it was just to remember them, like they should be remembered.

Or maybe it was to help.

Either way, I'm happy this family found their way into my life. Heaven will take you, Captain Sibley. You just have to ask again. Rest in peace, my friend.

As for the cemetery and the land beneath it, the earth remembers and pays a solemn tribute to all the souls who walked upon it.

Joni Mayhan is a paranormal investigator and the author of more than a dozen of books, including *Bones in the Basement: Surviving the S.K. Pierce Haunted Victorian Mansion*. To learn more about Mayhan, please visit her website: JoniMayhan.com.

CEMETERY DANGERS

Always be respectful when you visit. If you don't, you could be risking your own sanity. You won't want any of these entities following you home.
—Joni Mayhan, author of "Ghost Magnet" and "Signs of Spirits"

For many people, cemeteries are tranquil places where the dead can rest in peace. For others, it's the place where nightmares are manufactured. If you decide to explore these dangerously haunted cemeteries, know that you do so at your own risk. You might not like the consequences.

According to Shaman Michael Robishaw, most of the ghosts you encounter in cemeteries aren't the souls of the people who are buried there. Robishaw, who often helps people remove unwanted hauntings from their homes, feels that darker energies often loom there in hopes of finding easy prey.

I didn't always heed his advice and often found myself with unwanted house guests after spending time in cemeteries. One time, the attachment was so troublesome, it began affecting my health and tormenting my pets. It took weeks to finally remove it from my home.

Typically, most people cross over into the light when they die. They only remain earthbound if their death was a tragedy or they were fearful of their fate. If they committed a horrific sin during their lifetime, they might worry that they can't cross to the light, so they remain as earthbound ghosts instead. Many of these ghosts are eager for a host to attach to, so always be cautious when visiting cemeteries. You certainly don't want to run into one that is looking for a new home.

Bring your blessed medals and say a prayer before you go in and after you leave. Some people find that burning sage after visiting a cemetery helps disconnect the attachment. Just know that even if you are prepared, you could still end up with an unwanted hitchhiker.

If you still plan to visit one, just be forewarned that you might get more than you bargained for.

The following cemeteries have known hauntings and cautions you might wish to heed.

Union Cemetery in Easton, Connecticut was the subject of Ed and Lorraine Warren's book called *Graveyard. Photo by Frank C. Grace.*

UNION CEMETERY
EASTON, CONNECTICUT

This cemetery is so absurdly haunted, Ed and Lorraine Warren, the world-renown demonologists, wrote a book about it, entitled *Graveyard*. Located in southeastern Connecticut, near the New York border, this cemetery dates back to the early 1700s.

People often report seeing a White Lady roaming the cemetery grounds. Dressed in a white nightgown and bonnet, she has been described as having long dark hair, and has been also seen in the roadway along Route 59. Some say she also haunts the Stepney Cemetery in nearby Monroe, Connecticut and is believed to be spending her time walking back and forth between the two graveyards.

While no one knows who she is for certain, many people speculate that the White Lady is the ghost of a woman who was murdered after slaying her husband in the 1940s. Others contest she is the apparition of a woman who was brutally murdered in the early 1900s and dumped in a ditch near the cemetery.

Other sightings in the cemetery are far spookier. People have witnessed glowing red eyes peering at them from the darkness. Many believe it is the specter of Earle Kellog, who died after being set afire across the street in 1935.

CEMETERY DANGERS: Always pay attention while driving past this cemetery. Several motorists have nearly gotten into accidents after the White Lady suddenly appeared in the middle of the road before them. One person pulled off to the side after the sighting, finding a mysterious dent in his car from the impact with the dead woman.

DEAN HILL ROAD CEMETERY
FITCHBURG, MASSACHUSETTS

The Dean Hill Road Cemetery, known locally as "The Rev," due to its numerous Revolutionary War graves, is rife with legends. Located down a long, narrow dead-end road, the stage is set far before you arrive at your destination.

People who visit the cemetery have heard blood-curdling screams which seem to come from everywhere. Some say satanic rites were performed in the woods surrounding the desolate cemetery, causing the area to become deadly quiet for several years. People who visited were so unnerved by the absence of insect, bird and animal sounds, they left shortly afterwards.

Several deaths have occurred in the area, including a boy who supposedly burned to death and a woman who died in a car accident near the entrance. Two teens reportedly disappeared after becoming frightened in the cemetery. When they raced to their car, it wouldn't start, so they fled on foot, never to be seen again.

CEMETERY DANGERS: There was a headstone inside the cemetery that reads: "Ye who stands upon thy grave, shall soon follow." According to the legends, if you stand on the grave in front of this stone, you will soon face your own death. The stone has been stolen and returned three times, relocated in various places in the cemetery. It was stolen a fourth time and still remains missing. If it reappears, like some ghostly specter, don't tempt fate by standing in front of it.

ELDER BALLOU CEMETERY
CUMBERLAND, RHODE ISLAND

This small Rhode Island cemetery is tucked away on a hill, with graves dating back to the 1700s. As you approach it, the first thing you might notice is a row of stone crypts built into the hill, with a row of doorways facing the road, looking like a macabre motel of death. It's not difficult to let your mind wander as you stare at the closed doors, wondering what lurks in the dark shadows inside.

Visitors to the cemetery report feeling as though they are being watched. The cemetery has an abandoned forlorn feeling to it, with unkempt grounds and shaggy bushes growing in a haphazard manner. Visitors have reported seeing the apparition of a man in grey wandering the grounds. If approached, he will vanish into thin air.

CEMETERY DANGERS: According to one visitor, going to the cemetery after dark could have terrifying consequences. As she walked through the rugged terrain, stepping around the old gravestones, she began hearing footsteps behind her. When she stopped, the footsteps stopped, and when she ran, they raced on her heels until she was safely inside her car. She was thankful to make it home without a ghostly hitchhiker. Others haven't been so fortunate.

PINE HILL CEMETERY
HOLLIS, NEW HAMPSHIRE

Imagine driving past a cemetery at dusk and seeing a small child run out into the road ahead of you, vanishing into thin air as you stop the car. According to local legend, the little boy escaped the mass murder of his entire family, only to be gunned down in the road outside the cemetery as he attempted to flee. People have been witnessing his apparition for years.

Although this cemetery is closed at night, thrill seekers and paranormal enthusiasts proclaim this to be one of the most haunted cemeteries in New England. Dark shadows have been seen drifting through the gravestones and voices have been heard, calling out in the darkness. Some visitors have witnessed tombstones morphing in front of their eyes. Was it a trick of the eye or something altogether creepier?

Another reason for the haunting could be attributed to Abel Blood, whose family name provides the cemetery with its nickname of Blood Cemetery. According to legend, Abel Blood supposedly haunts the cemetery, looking for his wife Betsy. Some say that Abel was a practitioner of the dark arts and now spends his days in Heaven and his nights in Hell. The finger on his tombstone has been seen pointing downward during the night, while it points upwards during the day.

CEMETERY DANGERS: Visit this cemetery at night at your own risk. People who have attempted this have been chased out of the cemetery by unseen forces that left them shaken and unnerved. Once they got to their vehicles, they frequently discovered mechanical issues, with the car's electronics, but also to their cameras and cell phones.

OLD BURYING YARD
YORK, MAINE

The sight of crows in a graveyard often causes people to shudder, but in the case of the Old Burying Yard in York, Maine, it could have a far more sinister meaning.

The grave of Mary Nasson is different from all the other graves. Consisting of a headstone and a footstone, the grave also has one unusual feature: a slab of stone connecting the two.

Some speculate that the slab is there to keep animals from digging up the grave, but locals have a far creepier theory. They believe it was placed there to keep Mary from climbing out of her grave. Considering that Mary was an herbalist as well as an exorcist, local town people considered her to be a witch. The crows that flock to the cemetery are known as the White Witch of York's familiars, something you do not want to cross.

The cemetery also houses the remains from the 1692 Raid of York, where one hundred English settlers were murdered and their houses burned by angry natives. Gravestones in this quaint cemetery often give people an unsettled feeling. One stone reads: "Adieu my Friends, dry up your tears. I must lie here till Christ appears."

CEMETERY DANGERS: Children who visit the playground across the street from the cemetery have reported being pushed on the swings by the gentle hand of a woman who soon disappears into thin air. While she doesn't seem to impose any hostility, this isn't something most parents would like their children to experience. Many theorize that the ghost of Mary Naason is the culprit. Dying young at twenty-nine-years-old, she never got to experience motherhood. Perhaps she's simply following her maternal urges after death, but I still wouldn't want to experience it firsthand.

VALE END CEMETERY
WILTON, NEW HAMPSHIRE

The legends surrounding the Vale End Cemetery could fill a dozen horror movies. Perhaps the most haunting story surrounds the Blue Lady, thought to be the ghost of Mary Spaulding.

The mysteries surrounding Spaulding's death are numerous. Some say she was murdered by her own husband after a violent argument, while others claim she was killed by a satanic cult as part of a ceremony. Despite the method of her death, it was enough to keep her earthbound and restless. She often appears as a blue mist, hovering over her own grave.

Other people have witnessed the ghost of an older man near the gates of the cemetery. Locals say he buried his daughter at the cemetery decades ago. When her body was moved to another location, he began his eternal search for her, roaming the cemetery grounds in the darkness of the night.

CEMETERY DANGERS: This cemetery is one of the more dangerous locations on the list. Besides the Blue Lady and the older man, the cemetery is also frequented by a Pukwudgie. This two-to-three foot hairy creature has been known to show itself to nighttime visitors, lurking at the edges of the darkness as it stalks its human prey. Pukwudgies are tricksters with a vile sense of humor, often attempting to lure people to their deaths. One story tells of a woman who visited the cemetery with friends and witnessed a dark creature crawl out of one of the graves. She fled the cemetery, but was certain that a dark entity followed her home. According to the legend, she was found dead in her car in a busy parking lot days later, with no signs of trauma. Was she scared to death? I don't know, but I wouldn't even chance visiting this cemetery.

CONCLUSION: With any of these cemeteries, always abide by the local laws, respecting their wishes for their dead and buried. Always keep in mind that not all of the souls lingering here are benevolent. Some of them are simply lost and afraid, retreating from the prying eyes of thrill seekers. Always be respectful when you visit. If you don't, you could be risking your own sanity. You won't want any of these entities following you home.

Joni Mayhan is a paranormal investigator and the author of more than a dozen of books, including *Ghost Magnet* and *Signs of Spirits*. To learn more about Mayhan, please visit her website: JoniMayhan.com.

Scene from the movie *1408*? Author Sam Baltrusis unlocks the secrets hidden in New England's blood-stained hotels including the Providence Biltmore. *Photo by Jason Baker*

HAUNTED HOTELS

Looking for a hotel while exploring the most haunted cemeteries in Massachusetts? Check out the book "13 Most Haunted Hotels & Inns of New England" by author Sam Baltrusis. Here's an excerpt:

Want to see if a "room with a boo" is truly haunted? Work the graveyard shift at an allegedly haunted hotel.

For a few months in 2017, I signed on as a night auditor at two boo-tique inns, including the Hotel 140 in the Back Bay. Right above the front desk is the Lyric Stage Company theater. Multiple times in the wee hours of the night, I encountered a female spirit who'd mysteriously try to lead me upstairs. I'm not sure what her deal was, but she was desperately trying to communicate with me.

One Monday night in May 2017 when I was working the overnight shift at Hotel 140, I met Lyric Stage Company of Boston's associate production manager, Stephanie Hettrick. We started chatting, and within the first few minutes, she revealed to me that my hunch was true: the former YWCA turned hotel is in fact haunted. "We call her Alice," Hettrick said, speaking quietly so her friend couldn't hear her talking about the building's resident ghost. "She doesn't like me, but she likes my boss. He was away for a week and caused all sorts of problems. Things would mysteriously move. Lights would turn on and off. We blamed it on Alice."

When I asked her if she knew anything about Alice's backstory, Hettrick said she strongly believed the female spirit was in her early to late twenties. I asked her how she knew so many details about the resident spirit, and the production manager smiled. "Because I've seen her," she said, pointing to the second-floor mezzanine level of the hotel and the side-stairs area Alice is known to frequent. "She's wearing white, and sometimes when I'm here late at night in the theater, I will see her out of the corner of my eye."

Hettrick's friend, who was in the ladies' room behind Hotel 140's front desk, ran out in a tizzy. "Are you talking about ghosts? If you are then I'm going to leave now." Her friend was joking, but you could see she was obviously creeped out by the hotel's resident spirit.

Of course, Hotel 140 isn't the only overnight haunt in the Boston area that's reported to have supernatural activity. Several of the Hub's haunted dormitories, including Boston University's Kilachand Hall (formerly Shelton Hall and my sophomore-year college dorm) and Berklee College of Music's 150 Massachusetts Ave., had former lives as hotels. The Charlesgate, Emerson College's "devilish dormitory," which has been converted into upscale condominiums, was built in 1891 as a fin de siècle hotel and boasted upscale accommodations for Boston's elite and then deteriorated during the Depression before housing college students.

When it comes to haunted dorms, school spirits reflect school spirit. Based on my experience as a paranormal researcher and as the author of eight historical-based ghost books, I've unwittingly become a voice for New England's spirit squad. *We got spirits, yes we do.*

While writing the book on haunted hotels, I was featured on two national paranormal TV shows, including Destination America's *Haunted Towns*, which focused on Salem. I also made a cameo on the Travel Channel recounting my face-to-face encounter with a lady in white in the Witch City's Old Burying Point on Charter Street. In 2012, I was featured as Boston's paranormal expert on the Biography Channel's *Haunted Encounters.*

How can one person have so many experiences of New England's ghosts? I'm mysteriously called to these haunted locations. It's both a blessing and a curse.

Some of my paranormal friends are "ghost magnets." I don't necessarily attract or repel things that go bump in the night. My gift is that I intuitively know where the spirits are, and I inexplicably find myself in those places. Usually I end up in locations that aren't necessarily known to be haunted but turn out to be extremely active from a paranormal perspective.

I guess I have built-in "ghostdar."

In addition to my part-time gig at Hotel 140, my built-in ghost GPS led me to a hotel that's close to one of my favorite local haunts, the USS *Constitution* in the Boston Navy Yard. A stone's throw from the extremely active "Old Ironsides," the Constitution Inn had an under-the-radar paranormal reputation of sorts thanks to its close proximity to U.S. Navy's crown jewel, Charlestown's iconic wooden-hulled, three-masted heavy frigate.

When I first applied to be the hotel's part-time night auditor, my future boss nodded when I asked if the Constitution Inn had any resident ghosts. "Talk to the ladies in housekeeping," my manager said with a sheepish smile. "They swear they've seen something downstairs."

After several overnights working at the Constitution Inn, I invited several friends to investigate with me at the hotel, which included a visit to the supposedly haunted laundry room. It was a spirited night to say the least.

One of the guests, Cynthia Olson Mattison, had a weird communication during the investigation led by the S.P.I.R.I.T.S. of New England team at the Constitution Inn. Someone or something typed "hi" on her phone when she left it on the table. It was very strange and the beginning of communications with two possible spirits at the inn.

"We know for a fact there are other buildings within the Navy Yard that have activity," explained Jack Kenna, investigator with S.P.I.R.I.T.S. of New England. "Back in July of 2010 when we investigated the *Constitution*, some of the ship's officers told us about several other locations in the shipyard they had experiences in and believed were haunted," Kenna continued. "There's a lot of history in Charlestown and, of course, the entire Boston area. Some of that history goes all the way back to the 1600s. I do believe that this part of Boston could very well hold some of the most interesting and intense paranormal activity in the Boston area."

Kenna and Ellen MacNeil gave a spine-tingling lecture about their investigation on board the USS *Constitution*. During their discussion at the Constitution Inn, the door leading into the conference room mysteriously swung open and then closed.

Was it a spirit? Perhaps. I do know that somewhere deep in our subconscious, ghost stories satiate a primitive desire to know that life exists after death. Based on my experience working overnights at two potentially haunted hotels, I do believe that inns have a proclivity for hauntings based purely on the numbers of people who pass through them. Extreme emotions leave a psychic imprint. An intense moment—like a murder, suicide or even a wedding—could leave an indelible mark.

However, the residual haunting theory apparently doesn't apply to all of New England's historic overnight haunts. If I had to choose one hotel in New England that I thought would be haunted but isn't, it would be Boston's Liberty Hotel. Based purely on its history, the Hub's "most wanted" should also be Boston's most haunted. But it's not.

Located at 215 Charles St., Boston's posh Liberty Hotel had a past life as the Charles Street Jail. But is it haunted? *Photo courtesy of the Boston Public Library, Print Department.*

The Liberty Hotel—formerly the Charles Street Jail, which housed a rogues' gallery of former clientele, including several mob bosses; a German U-boat captain who killed himself with shards from his sunglasses soon after being captured in 1945; Frank Abagnale Jr., the notorious con artist played by Leonardo DiCaprio in the flick *Catch Me If You Can*; and Boston mayor James Michael Curley, who served time for fraud in 1904—was reborn as a luxury hotel in 2007. However, have the ghosts from the jail's dodgy past left the massive gray granite and brick structure since closing its doors in 1990?

Some guests aren't convinced. "When I told my husband about this place, he looked at me like I was nuts. I don't know if we'll ever actually stay at The Liberty, as it has to be haunted, and I'm a big chicken," wrote Paloma Contrera from *High Gloss Magazine*. "One hundred fifty plus years of poor living conditions for angry criminals... That is a sure-fire recipe for mean ghosts."

When the jail opened in 1851, it was praised as a world-class model of prison architecture. Built in the shape of a cross, the Charles Street Jail had a ninety-foot-high central rotunda and four wings of cells. In the late 1880s, each of the 220 rooms housed one inmate. However, things changed as the jail aged and fell into disrepair. In the 1970s, a riot broke out, and inmates sued over the building's squalid, overcrowded conditions. A federal judge ordered the structure closed in 1973, but it took seventeen years for many of the prisoners to find new homes. After a five-year, $150 million renovation, the former lockup reopened as the Liberty Hotel, which tipped its hat to the building's captivating but dark past with a restaurant called Clink and a bar named Alibi. However, only eighteen of the hotel's 298 rooms are housed in the building's original jail.

In an attempt to rid the building of any negative residual energy haunting the hotel, management brought in a team of Buddhist monks to perform a cleansing ritual. "Clearly, there are some very dark and depressing elements to this building, and we have to be careful how we tell its story," said Stuart Meyerson, former general manager, in the British newspaper *The Independent*. "I don't think everyone enjoyed staying here."

Former Liberty Hotel patron Charlene Swauger of Albuquerque believed the cleansing ritual worked. "I didn't discover any ghosts or anything," she told the *Associated Press*. "I thought it was very clever."

As far as lingering spirits are concerned, the Liberty's former marketing manager insisted that no shadow figures can be seen walking the iron-railing balconies, which were once catwalks where guards stood watch over the inmates. "Believe it or not, there have been no unusual occurrences here at the hotel," she told me.

However, tour buses passing by the 150-year-old structure allude to the Liberty's spirited past, including a mention that the hotel's courtyard was formerly a gallows, and travel journalists play with the Charles Street Jail's creepy vibe. "The Liberty Hotel, Boston's reconfigured former jail, once housed characters like the Boston Strangler," mused the *Austin American-Statesman* in an article called "Boston's Scariest Haunts" in October 2010. "Guests say they gather in the lobby champagne bar just because there's always safety in numbers."

Yes, the Liberty Hotel has a macabre past. It should be haunted, but it's not.

A handful of potential locations in New England didn't make the *13 Most Haunted* list because they're technically not inns or hotels … they're lighthouses. At least two haunts available for overnight stays—Rose Island Lighthouse in Newport, Rhode Island and Borden Flats Light in Fall River, Massachusetts— reportedly have lingering spirits.

Built in 1870, the Rose Island Lighthouse in Newport's Narragansett Bay is said to be home to former keeper Charles Curtis who still opens and closes doors even though his last day on the job was in 1918. Visitors who take a ferry to Rose Island can even spend the night in the allegedly haunted barracks formerly used to quarantine dysentery victims. Over at Borden Flats Light in Fall River, paranormal investigators have reported what sounded like a man whistling and a little girl laughing. Sensitives claim that Captain John Paul, keeper of the Borden Flats Light between 1912–1927, continues to keep watch in the afterlife.

Haunted lighthouses? Yes, it's a no-brainer.

Jeremy D'Entremont, author and historian of the American Lighthouse Foundation, jokingly told me that people can find at least one ghost story associated with each of the dozens of lighthouses scattered throughout New England if they dig deep enough.

"Just imagine living at an isolated, offshore lighthouse all year round, through storms and all kinds of extreme conditions," he told me. "Such an existence could easily cause the imagination to play tricks. But I do believe that many of these stories are at least partially true. Some people think that the ocean is a good conductor of paranormal energy. I'm not sure about that, but lighthouses are among the oldest structures in many of our coastal communities, and their human history is dramatic and full of emotion."

The historian told me that he's heard several strange-but-true tales from the various structures. "Many of these stories seem to point to a lighthouse keeper of the past who continues to 'keep watch,' even after his death," he said.

D'Entremont, the go-to expert for New England lighthouses, said he even had a close encounter himself while giving a tour at his home haunt for fifteen years, Portsmouth Harbor Light in New Castle, New Hampshire. "One day I was giving a tour for a married couple in the middle of the afternoon. We were at the top of the stairs, in the watch room. I was leaning against a ladder and telling them some of the history of the place," he recalled. "As I was talking, a low, gravelly, male voice from my right said, 'Hello.' I stopped and asked the couple if they'd heard anything."

The husband in the group swore he also heard a man say "hello," whereas his wife didn't hear a peep. "We looked down the stairs and outside, and there was nobody else anywhere near the lighthouse. A few other people have had similar experiences," he added.

Of course, D'Entremont said extreme isolation could factor into each alleged ghost sighting. "I definitely think living at a remote, isolated location can play tricks on your imagination," he continued. "I have no doubt that some ghost stories were based on strange but natural sights and sounds experienced by the keepers and their families. I also think that keepers and family members shared stories, and they are prone to exaggeration as they're passed down."

The Borden Flats Light is a historic and potentially haunted lighthouse on the Taunton River in Fall River, Massachusetts. *Photo by Frank C. Grace.*

As far as my personal experiences writing *13 Most Haunted Hotels and Inns of New England* are concerned, my abilities as an empath gradually heightened over the two-year period I spent visiting these extremely haunted hotels. When I first started, I felt like John Cusack's character Mike Enslin in the movie *1408*. I was still somewhat of a skeptic. However, I had several life-changing experiences with the paranormal along the way.

When I visited Fall River's iconic murder house, the Lizzie Borden B&B, I was expecting to be underwhelmed. I wasn't. In fact, within the first few minutes, I spotted a shadow figure dart past, and I connected deeply with Lizzie Borden's stepmother, Abby, in the John Morse room. I was in tears when I walked over to the scene of the crime.

Sue Vickery, a tour guide at the Lizzie Borden B&B, said my sensitivities were spot on. "Yes, it's a very common experience," she told me. "I've also been overcome with sadness on occasion in that room. I've had guests walk through that doorway and break out in tears."

Vickery, who was recently featured on TLC's *Kindred Spirits* with Amy Bruni and Adam Berry, said the hauntings at the Lizzie Borden B&B live up to the building's national reputation. "The Bordens are very much still a presence here," she said. "I've spoken with Andrew, Abby, Lizzie and occasionally Emma through the spirit box. I've witnessed black mist and white mist. I've had voices speak when no one is in the house. Footsteps are common. Doors open and close. I've been touched on numerous occasions as well."

In addition to my visit to the Lizzie Borden B&B, my most profound personal experience occurred during an overnight stay at Captain Grant's Inn in Preston, Connecticut. I somehow channeled the spirit of the inn's resident gay ghost, Liam. I first connected with him during an impromptu interview with the innkeeper, Carol Matsumoto, in the kitchen. During our chat, it felt as if someone hugged me from behind. Matsumoto jokingly said, "oh, that's just Liam," and I mused that Liam needed to learn a thing or two about boundaries.

I immediately felt connected with him as he led me to an open field behind the historic structure. During my trek out to the cemetery hidden behind the inn, I touched a tree, and it felt as if I was being transported back in time. Based on my vision, Liam loved to fish, and he was attacked by the locals for being different. He desperately wanted to tell me his story. I was standing in the middle of the field, shivering in the beauty and the madness of the moment.

After connecting with Liam, I headed inside and immediately passed out. It was a deep sleep in which I experienced full-blown spirit communication with the inn's resident ghosts. In the dream, I was hanging out with Liam, and he was wearing an outfit that appeared to be from the eighteenth century.

The following morning during breakfast, Carol asked me if I was out fishing in the brook behind the cemetery. I was shocked. Fishing? "Yes, we thought we saw you out there with a fishing pole." I'm not into fishing, but Liam definitely was. I held my breath.

CONCLUSION

"Cemeteries have a lot of activity. The [spirits] want to talk to you, and they may have a story to pass on, Cemeteries are where they go to rest and don't want to be bothered."

—*Adam Berry, TV's "Kindred Spirits"*

One night, when I was setting up for a book signing at the church next to Cambridge's Old Burying Point, I had a close encounter with an unseen force. The back door, which was oddly propped open by one of the cemetery's old-school gravestones, mysteriously closed. I heard what sounded like the floorboards creaking and then a second door slammed shut. I looked up and spotted something, or someone, out of the corner of my eye. He looked like a Revolutionary War–era soldier, and he was wearing a tricorn hat. I held my breath.

At this point, I didn't know about the legend surrounding Lieutenant Richard Brown, a British soldier who was shot in the face in 1777 by a Patriot sentry while descending Prospect Hill in Somerville. He was buried in the Vassall tomb and allegedly haunts Christ Church, which also abuts the Old Burying Ground. Apparently, his interment was so controversial that hundreds of crazed colonists ransacked the historic Anglican church. Brown's spirit reportedly comes up, slams doors and blows out candles.

Did you know that a "graveyard" is typically associated with a church and a "cemetery" is more of general term for a burial ground? *Photo by Frank C. Grace.*

Was my encounter at the church a ghost? Not sure. However, I do believe in residual hauntings or a videotape-like replay of a traumatic event that occurred years ago. My theory is that Cambridge's Old Burying Ground is full of skeletal secrets, an energy vortex of unjust killings and unmarked graves dating back to the days leading up to the Revolutionary War.

For several years, I produced a ghost tour called Cambridge Haunts and we had repeated sightings and hard-to-explain photos shot in the area believed to be Cambridge's haunted corridor. Most of the guides on the ghost walk agreed Cambridge Haunt's starting point, the Old Burying Point, was one of the most active spots on the tour.

If I had an "honorable mention" for the *13 Most Haunted Cemeteries in Massachusetts* list, it would be the old graveyard next to the historic, and allegedly haunted, Christ Church.

Known for its prestigious universities, Cambridge became an unlikely hot spot in the days leading up to the Revolutionary War. However, there was little indication of this overnight upheaval in the early 1700s. Its Sleepy Hollow–esque vibe, modeled after the picturesque English villages its Puritan founders had left behind, turned into chaos as nine thousand citizen soldiers from rustic country towns scattered throughout New England gathered in the Cambridge Common in 1775. Before the "shot heard 'round the world" in Concord on April 29, Cambridge boasted about two thousand residents, 90 percent of whom were descendants of the seven hundred Puritans who had sailed from England to Newtowne in 1630.

According to legend, General George Washington assumed his role as commander of the thousands of militiamen known as the Continental army beneath an elm tree in the Common. This epic scene, which has been immortalized by illustrators and storytellers over the years, is believed to be more myth than fact. According to Richard Ketchum's *The World of George Washington*, the emerging leader was concerned with his crew of untrained militiamen, calling them a "mixed multitude of people…under very little discipline, order or government."

In other words, Washington had his work cut out for him.

The sudden upheaval in 1775 is believed to be the source of some of the residual energy that left a psychic imprint of sorts on the weathered streets and centuries-old buildings in Harvard Square. According to master psychic Denise Fix, a handful of Cambridge's ghosts can be traced back to the Revolutionary War. "Some of the spirits around us are wearing uniforms," said Fix during a visit to Cambridge's Old Burying Ground. "There's a lot of residual energy associated with men from George Washington's era. I keep seeing men wearing [tricorn] hats."

The precursor to the American Revolutionary War, known as the Battle of Lexington and Concord in April 1775, claimed the lives of six Cantabrigians. Oddly, they weren't killed during the battle but during the British retreat. Two locals, Jabez Wyman and Jason Winship, were downing a few ales at Cooper's Tavern, which is located near Beech Street in North Cambridge.

"The King's regular troops under the command of General [Thomas] Gage, upon their return from blood and slaughter, which they had made at Lexington and Concord, fired more than one hundred bullets into the house where we dwell, through doors and windows," recalled Rachel Cooper, who ran the tavern with her husband, Benjamin, in an interview one month after the horrific incident. "The two aged gentlemen were immediately most barbarously and inhumanly murdered by them, being stabbed through in many places, their heads mangled, skulls broke and their brains out on the floor and walls of the house."

Both Wyman and Winship were buried in Cambridge's Old Burying Ground in Harvard Square.

John Hicks, a diehard Patriot who trekked eight miles to participate in the Boston Tea Party, also died in April 1775 as the British marched in full retreat toward Boston. Trying to launch a surprise attack against the redcoats, Hicks hid behind some barrels at Watson's Corner in North Cambridge. He was joined by Moses Richardson and Isaac Gardner, the first Harvard graduate (class of 1747) who died for liberty. They all were bayoneted by the redcoats, and Hicks was shot through the heart. Williams Marcy, who thought he was seeing a parade, was shot as he sat on a wall and cheered.

"Hicks, Richardson and Marcy were buried in an unmarked grave and were soon forgotten as Cambridge became an armed camp of several thousand minutemen gathered from all over New England to oppose the British," reported the Cambridge Historical Commission. "In 1875, the Patriot's common grave was found in the Old Burying Ground and monuments were erected there and in front of the Watson house at 2154 Massachusetts Ave." Today, there's a concrete marker commemorating what was Cambridge's version of the Boston Massacre.

Hicks, who was among the casualties from the era, lived in what is currently Harvard's Kirkland House library. Israel Putnam—who spearheaded the Battle of Bunker Hill and is arguably one of the more colorful officers of the Revolution, thanks to folklore from his youth that suggested he killed the last wolf in Connecticut—moved into the Hicks house, which was built in 1762 and is located across from Winthrop Park in Harvard Square.

Are the ghosts of Cambridge's Revolutionary War past still hanging out in the area? It's possible. Paranormal investigators like Adam Berry from *Kindred Spirits* believe that residual energy associated with this tumultuous time in American history may have left a supernatural imprint. "Anytime there's a traumatic event, it could be left behind," Berry said. "If you walk into a room and two people have been arguing, fiercely, you can feel that weirdness that they've created or energy they emit spewing at each other. I do think there's a form of energy that can be left behind from a traumatic event or any kind of murder or suicide in a room. The theory is that maybe that energy goes into the walls and lingers there."

When it comes to the ghosts of Cambridge's past, all paths lead to the corner of Massachusetts Avenue and Garden Street. Known as "God's Acre," the Old Burying Ground was established before 1635 and preceded both Christ Church and First Parish. Harvard presidents and paupers were buried there. Paranormal investigators, like Adam Berry from TLC's *Kindred Spirits*, believe the older the cemetery, the more intimidating. "Cemeteries are where they go to rest and don't want to be bothered," Berry told me. "I don't believe they're bound or held captive in that specific spot. However, I do feel they're abundant."

The city of Cambridge was known as Newtowne until 1638, and the town's oldest cemetery was rumored to be around Brattle and Ash Streets. It's long gone. "It was deemed that the cemetery was not safe from the intrusion of wild animals, and the cemetery was not used after 1634," wrote Roxie Zwicker in *Massachusetts Book of the Dead*. "There is no indication of where the cemetery is in the city today, as it has been lost to time and urban development."

As the only burial spot for nearly two hundred years, the Old Burying Ground received a cross section of the population, including slaves Neptune Frost and Cato Stedman and at least nineteen Revolutionary War soldiers. Burial spaces in the early years weren't permanently marked, and the cemetery contains many more remains than are in the 1,218 known graves. Most of the monuments are slate headstones, and some markers, including those crafted by Joseph Lamson from Charlestown, portray "evil demons of death" with imps carrying coffins away. The oldest gravestone, dated 1653, belongs to Anne Erinton, but the stone may have been placed later, as headstones didn't come into general use until the 1670s. Excluding the tombs, the cemetery's last known burial was in 1811.

There's also a subterranean tunnel. As in Britain, upper-class families wished to be interred in burial vaults rather than in caskets placed directly in the ground. The John Vassall tomb is the most elaborate. Last opened in 1862, it contained twenty-five caskets, including that of Andrew Craigie, who acquired the family's Christ Church pew and burial plot along with the Vassall estate in 1792.

Mythology surrounding the Vassall family continues to polarize historians. Penelope Vassall, who fled Cambridge during the Revolutionary War, supposedly paid twenty pounds in 1722 to free the child of her driver Tony from slavery. "Cambridge, becoming a military camp, was neither a pleasant nor safe residence for those who still adhered to King George, so Madame Vassall departed in haste to Antigua," wrote Dorothy Dudley in *Theatrum Majorum*. "Popular tradition asserts that the slaves of the Vassalls were inhumanely treated. There seems to be no foundation of this report." Penelope Vassall visited Cambridge after the Revolution and, after struggling financially, was buried in the subterranean vault beneath Christ Church. She was joined by Tony's son Darby Vassall, an African American man, who was eventually freed from slavery. He was the last person to be interred in the tomb on October 15, 1861.

Leave it to Cambridge to challenge the status quo.

The Old Burying Ground also boasts Harvard's first president, Henry Dunster, who was banished from Cambridge for challenging the Puritans' views on baptism. In 1654, he begged church authorities to allow his family to stay in the modest home he had built with his own money, but he was forced to move to Plymouth County and was replaced by Charles Chauncy, a local minister who believed in the faith-based tradition. Dunster's unorthodox views earned him an unsavory "Harvard heretic" moniker because he interrupted church services and declined to have his fourth child baptized. Puritan elders believed the Devil was working through the Harvard president, and after meeting with magistrates in Boston, he was forced to resign. The university's founding president, who lived the last five years of his life in Scituate, died a broken man in 1659. Dunster's last wish? He wanted to be buried in Cambridge, close to his beloved Harvard.

But is the Old Burying Ground haunted? Perhaps. Curiosity seekers on my former Cambridge Haunts ghost tour have snapped tons of photos with so-called orbs, and a few swear they've seen what looked like a full-bodied apparition. Master psychic Denise Fix, who visited the cemetery with the author, made contact with Seth Hastings, who passed on October 15, 1775. Fix said the "gentleman whose benevolence extended to all," as indicated by his gravestone, was itching to make contact with the living. According to Fix, Hastings was a cordial man with a sense of humor even though he's six feet under.

Berry, who spent hours in old cemeteries armed with an EVP recorder before auditioning for *Ghost Hunters Academy* and then officially joining TAPS (The Atlantic Paranormal Society) team and ultimately *Kindred Spirits,* said burial grounds attract spirits. "Cemeteries have a lot of activity. The [spirits] want to talk to you, and they may have a story to pass on," he remarked. "As investigators, we try not to go on feelings, because you can't prove feelings. But you can't ignore your biggest organ, which is your skin and the goose bumps that you get, and feeling like you're being watched."

SOURCES

I updated excerpts from my first four books including *Ghosts of Boston*: *Haunts of the Hub* and *Ghosts of Salem*: *Haunts of the Witch City* and *13 Most Haunted in Massachusetts* were featured in *13 Most Haunted Cemeteries in Massachusetts*. The material in this book is drawn from published sources, including issues of *the Eagle-Tribune*, *Boston Globe*, *Boston Herald*, *Wicked Local*, *The New York Times*, *Patriot Ledger*, *SouthCoast Today* and television programs like the Travel Channel's *Ghost Adventures* and Destination America's *Haunted Towns*. Several books on the Bay State's paranormal history were used and cited throughout the text. Other New England–based websites and periodicals, like my various newspaper and magazine articles on the paranormal, Joni Mayhan's work for *Ghost Diaries* and Peter Muise's blog *New England Folklore* served as primary sources. I also conducted first-hand interviews, and some of the material is drawn from my own research. The Boston-based ghost tour, Boston Haunts, was also a major source and generated original content. My tours in Salem, Cambridge and Boston Harbor also served as inspiration for the book. It should be noted that ghost stories are subjective, and I have made a concerted effort to stick to the historical facts, even if it resulted in debunking an alleged encounter with the paranormal.

Baltrusis, Sam. *Ghosts of Boston: Haunts of the Hub*. Charleston, SC: The History Press, 2012.

Baltrusis, Sam. *Ghosts of Cambridge: Haunts of Harvard Square and Beyond*. Charleston, SC: The History Press, 2013.

Baltrusis, Sam. *Ghosts of Salem: Haunts of the Witch City*. Charleston, SC: The History Press, 2014.

D'Agostino, Thomas. *A Guide to Haunted New England*. Charleston, SC: The History Press, 2009.

Forest, Christopher. *North Shore Spirits of Massachusetts*. Atglen, PA: Schiffer Publishing, 2003.

Gellerman, Bruce and Sherman, Erik. *Massachusetts Curiosities*. Guilford, CT: The Globe Pequot Press, 2005.

Hall, Thomas. *Shipwrecks of Massachusetts Bay*. Charleston, SC: The History Press, 2012.

Hauk, Dennis William. *Haunted Places: The National Directory.* New York: Penguin Group, 1996.

Jasper, Mark. *Haunted Cape Cod & The Islands.* Yarmouthport, MA: On Cape Publications, 2002.

Mayhan, Joni. *Dark and Scary Things.* Gardner, MA: Joni Mayhan, 2015.

Muise, Peter. *Legends and Lore of the North Shore.* Charleston, SC: The History Press, 2014.

Nadler, Holly Mascott. *Ghosts of Boston Town: Three Centuries of True Hauntings.* Camden, ME: Down East Books, 2002.

Norman, Michael and Scott, Beth. *Historic Haunted America.* New York, NY: Tor Books, 1995.

Ogden, Tom. *The Complete Idiot's Guide to Ghosts & Hauntings.* Indianapolis, IN: Alpha Books, 2004.

Revai, Cheri. *Haunted Massachusetts: Ghosts and Strange Phenomena of the Bay State.* Mechanicsburg, PA: Stackpole Books, 2005.

ABOUT THE AUTHOR

Sam Baltrusis, author of the best-selling *Ghosts of Salem: Haunts of the Witch City*, has penned nine historical-based ghost books. He has been featured on several national TV shows including Destination America's *Haunted Towns*, the Travel Channel's *Haunted USA* on Salem and served as Boston's paranormal expert on the Biography Channel's *Haunted Encounters*. Baltrusis moonlights as a tour guide and launched the successful ghost tours, Boston Haunts, Graveyard Getaways and the Wicked Salem tour. He also led tours with several heritage organizations including the House of the Seven Gables and Essex Heritage. Baltrusis is a sought-after lecturer who speaks at dozens of paranormal-related events scattered throughout New England, including an author discussion at the Massachusetts State House and a paranormal convention he produced in 2018 called the Plymouth ParaCon. In the past, he has worked for VH1, MTV.com, *Newsweek* and ABC Radio and as a regional stringer for the *New York Times*. Visit SamBaltrusis.com for more information.

Doppelgänger? Author Sam Baltrusis specializes in historical haunts and has been featured on several national television shows sharing his experiences with the paranormal. *Photo by Frank C. Grace.*

Made in United States
North Haven, CT
10 April 2022

18101834R00063